# GETTING A GRIP

# ALSO BY FRANCES MOORE LAPPÉ

Liberation Ecology: Reframing Six Disempowering Ideas that Keep Us from Aligning with Nature—Even Our Own

Democracy's Edge: Choosing to Save Our Country by Bringing Democracy to Life

You Have the Power: Choosing Courage in a Culture of Fear (with Jeffrey Perkins)

Hope's Edge: The Next Diet for a Small Planet (with Anna Lappé)

The Quickening of America: Rebuilding Our Nation, Remaking Our Lives (with Paul Martin Du Bois)

Diet for a Small Planet

Taking Population Seriously (with Rachel Schurman)

Rediscovering America's Values

Betraying the National Interest (with Rachel Schurman and Kevin Danaher)

World Hunger: Twelve Myths (with Joseph Collins, Peter Rosset and Luis Esparza)

What To Do After You Turn Off the T.V.

Nicaragua: What Difference Could a Revolution Make? (with Joseph Collins and Paul Rice)

Now We Can Speak (with Joseph Collins)

Aid as Obstacle (with Joseph Collins and David Kinley)

Mozambique and Tanzania: Asking the Big Questions (with Adele Beccar-Varela)

Food First: Beyond the Myth of Scarcity (with Joseph Collins and Cary Fowler)

Great Meatless Meals (with Ellen Ewald)

FRANCES MOORE LAPPÉ

# GETTING A GRIP 2

clarity, creativity, and courage for the world we really want

A Small Planet Media Book



Social benefit organizations are encouraged to contact us about bulk discounts for their constituencies.

Richard R. Rowe, Ph. D., Publisher, Small Planet Media

Printed in the United States by Sterling Printing: member CWA local 13

Distributed by Publisher's Group West
First printing, October 2007
Second printing, February 2010

10 9 8 7 6 5 4 3 2

This book is printed with soy ink on acid-free recycled paper.

Publisher's Cataloging in Publication Data
Lappé, Frances Moore.
Getting a Grip 2: clarity, creativity and courage for the world we really want/ by Frances Moore Lappé
p. cm.
Includes biographical references and index.
ISBN-13: 978-0-9794142-3-7
ISBN-10: 0-9794142-3-7
1. Social participation. 2. Democracy.
3. Sustainable development I. Title

2010900419

Small Planet Media
25 Mt. Auburn St., Ste. 203
Cambridge, MA 02138
(617) 441-6300 x115
www.smallplanetmedia.org

*For democracy champion*
*Howard Zinn (1922-2010),*
*with the hope this work will help*
*to carry your bright torch*
*forward.*

# GETTING A GRIP 2

## clarity, creativity, and courage for the world we really want

## COURAGE

# IDEAS

to help us probe deeply, identify causal forces, choose entry points, and shift patterns

# ACKNOWLEDGEMENTS

This book reflects a life's quest, so by rights I should acknowledge all who have influenced my path. Here, at least, is a start.

First, I thank Richard Rowe, my partner, for the joy of our common exploration and your countless selfless acts of support and insight enabling this book. Likewise, my children Anthony and Anna Lappé and their spouses Clarice Lappé and John Marshall, whose encouragement and advice help keep me going.

At the Small Planet Institute, I am grateful for Julie Jensen and Brooke Ormond who deftly and cheerfully managed this project. Thank you also Nicole Crescimanno and Alex Tung for research support; and Samantha Mignotte for standing with me during the last big push.

I'm indebted to Jeffrey Perkins for our book, *You Have the Power*, which fed the chapter here on transforming fear. Thank you, readers of the first edition draft, who offered feedback: Diana Beliard, Gloria Foster, Ephraim Julius Freed, Michael Richardson, Walter Robb, Laura Shelton, and Jim Staton. For the first edition the Institute's Jess Wilson along with TeamDemocracy members, offered support for which I'm grateful. They include: Carolina Aparicio, Noah Joffe-Halpern, Michael Kowalski, Keith Lane, Erica Licht, Rebecca Mailman, Dani O'Brien, and Angela Smalley.

I appreciate the careful copyediting and proofing by Leah Goodwin and Joe Caliguire. For the book's lovely interior design, I'm indebted both to Chad Morgan for the first edition and Jamie Kerry for this edition. Thank you, Carol Maglitta, for a powerful cover design.

Other friends, and friends of this book, have helped enormously in keeping me focused. Thank you Hathaway Barry, Diana Beliard, Sue Bumagin, Jared Duval, Mark Finser, Maja Göepel, Bruce Haynes, Susan Kanaan, Miguel Mendonca, Josh Mailman, Rose Pritzker, Linda Pritzker, and Aaron Stern.

Finally, I am indebted to Harry Boyte and to Benjamin Barber, whose work on the themes of this book has helped open my eyes; and to Sarah Blaffer Hrdy, whose outstanding scholarship informs this new edition. Finally, the Industrial Areas Foundation's work to evolve concepts of power and public life have contributed to my understanding of Living Democracy.

—Frances Moore Lappé<br>
Cambridge, Massachusetts<br>
January 2010

# OPENING NOTE

It's Thanksgiving morning and I'm sitting at the kitchen table. This afternoon, thirty-three members of our extended family will arrive for dinner, and for hours afterward we'll circle in the living room, singing and laughing. Never has it felt easier than right now to count my personal blessings—finding the love of my life is but one on a long, long list.

I'd planned to start chopping the veggies, but instead I just sit. My mind moves to the arc of the decade now ending, and I feel a sharp sensation. Tears well up.

Not in despair, not in joy. No, I realize it's an awareness of the huge gap that's getting to me.

*The gap?*

I'll try to explain. In 1970, looking out on San Francisco Bay as I pounded away at the typewriter to compose *Diet for a Small*

*Planet*, I'd just been jolted into action by a basic fact: Hundreds of millions of people were going hungry, yet world harvests were more than enough to feed us all well.[1]

Now, as I begin this book four decades later, I realize that in just a few years the number of hungry people worldwide has grown by almost a fifth to over a billion—now well exceeding what had so disturbed me as a young woman.[2] Yet, production has more than kept pace with our growing population. Since I began counting, agricultural output per person has climbed by 20 percent.[3]

And while the decade in which I wrote my first book, the sixties, saw the U.S. poverty rate slashed in half, in the decade just ending the number of poor people grew each year by an average of *one million*, hitting a record high.[4] In 2008, the number of Americans so poor that even getting enough food to eat is a problem had, in just one year, climbed by a third.[5]

My unexpected emotion is a response, I realize, not only to these giant steps in the wrong direction, but to the huge gap between what we, humanity, now know about what works—and is *working* in so many places—and what we're doing that's not working.

I get up from the table and start chopping.

Don't get me wrong, though. Despite my tears on a happy day, I'm not bewildered or overwhelmed by our world gone mad. I'm ready. I'm *past* ready. I just want to go for it. Why can't we have a nation—why can't we have a world—we're proud of? Why can't we stop wringing our hands over poverty, hunger, species decimation, genocide, and death from curable disease that we know is all needless?

I now see there is no reason we can't.

They say—whoever "they" are—that as we age, we mellow. I don't think so. I'm getting less and less patient.

Why? Because I realize that humanity has no excuses anymore. In the span of my own lifetime, both historical evidence and breakthroughs in knowledge have wiped out all our excuses. We know how to end this needless suffering, and we have all the resources to do it. From sociology and anthropology to economics, from education and ecology to systems analysis, the evidence is in. We know what works.

Both "soft" psychology and "hard" neuroscience confirm that we humans come equipped with a moral compass—with deep needs and sensibilities that make us yearn to end the suffering. Yet we deny these feelings every single day at huge cost to our society and our world.

No physical obstacle is stopping us. Nothing. The barrier is in our heads. We are creating this world gone mad, not because we're compelled to by some deep flaws in our nature and not because Nature itself is stingy and unforgiving, but because of ideas we hold.

Ideas?

Yes. This is one of the most startling discoveries—awakenings—of the last century: Human beings are in fact creatures of the mind. Our ideas about reality determine what we see, what we believe is possible, and therefore what we become. And we also now know that human beings can change our big, life-shaping ideas, even our ideas of democracy, of power, of fear, and—yes—of evil itself.

As we do, we no longer have to settle for grasping at straws—wild acts of protest, or tearful acts of charity, or any other short-term, feel-less-bad steps. We become open to the possibility of real change. And, when you think about it, how could we ever believe the world can change unless we experience ourselves changing?

So this is what getting a grip means to me. It means learning to see the killer ideas that trap us and letting them go. It means people of all walks of life together interrupting the spiral of despair and reversing it with new ideas, ingenious innovation, and courage. It means finding that mixture of anger and hope to energize us for this do-or-die effort. Why not go for it?

Frances Moore Lappé
Cambridge, Massachusetts
January 2010

# PART 1
# CLARITY

# 1 A SPECIES GROWS UP

*Why are we as societies creating a world that we as individuals abhor?*

This is the question that's propelled my life. We know that no human being actually gets up in the morning vowing, "Yeah, today I'm going to make sure another child dies needlessly of hunger," or muttering, "Sure, I'll do my part to heat the planet and obliterate entire species."

Yet each day over twenty-four thousand young children die of hunger and poverty, and roughly one hundred more species are forever gone.[6] And the crises are not abating. They just keep whacking us: global climate chaos, terrorism, racial and religious divides, life-stunting poverty, and pandemic disease.

Again...why?

Unless we can answer this question—"Why are we creating a world no one wants?"—we can't have the world we do want. Only with a strong working theory about how we got here do we have real choice, the choice of something better. Without it, we're left paralyzed by despair or we're tempted to seize on any gesture of charity or protest—any random act of sanity. That way, for a moment at least, we can feel less useless in face of the magnitude of the crises.

But, unable to link our specific acts to real solutions, a sense of futility soon takes over.

Feeling powerless, we're robbed of energy and creativity, with hearts left open to fear, despair, and depression. No wonder the World Health Organization tells us depression is now the fourth leading cause of lost productive life worldwide—and is expected soon to jump to second place. Or that suicides worldwide now exceed homicides by 50 percent.[7]

For a lot of us, there is no real answer to the big "why." Things just keep happening. We know we're not in control, and it seems like nobody is.

In his poem "The World's One Hope," Bertolt Brecht laments that any one of us, seeing a child about to be struck by a car "pulls it onto the pavement," yet humanity fails to reach out to save the millions of children stricken by poverty and hunger every single day. Empathy, Brecht suggests, is our "one hope."

Brecht implies that inaction proves callousness. But I believe it proves something else: Mainly, we don't reach out to save the millions because we have no idea how this tragedy came to be or how it could ever end. *We feel powerless.*

But what if...what if...together with our friends, family, and acquaintances, we could probe the root causes of the biggest threats to our planet? What if we were able to grasp something of the common origins of these threats and then identify powerful entry points to interrupt them? More than that, what if we could then feel we are turning the underlying patterns toward life?

Now, that's power. Our power.

So let me take you along the path that brought me to my impatience. To start, let's look at some prevailing theories of why we're here, and possible assumptions beneath them. Perhaps, if we can dredge up the assumptions that we absorb unconsciously and examine them in the light of day, we can defuse their power and feel free to shape the new.

## WHAT IS OUR PROBLEM?

### It's the bad "other."

Maybe, although it's hard to say out loud even to ourselves, many of us assume that it's those bad people who got us here. *They* are doing this awful stuff—violence, hunger, economic pillage—to the rest of us. Badness may be in us all, sure, but there's really only enough to worry about in a minority—in *them*. We have this mad, sad world because we haven't yet been able get rid of, or at least sideline, them—the really evil ones.

For many, they include the greedy ones. "Greed kills. Greed is literally choking the life out of our country," writes former Goldman Sachs managing director Nomi Prins in *It Takes a Pillage*. Her wrath is directed at those financiers who brought the global economy to its knees.[8] It's hard not to share her rage when Goldman

Sachs' executives, along with other investment bankers, made billions marketing mortgage-backed securities based on a strong housing market while at the same time secretly betting that the housing market would tank.[9] Even as they insisted they couldn't possibly have seen the crash coming! (Those blaming the bankers weren't exactly mollified when Goldman Sachs' Lloyd Blankfein described his industry as doing "God's work.")[10]

In a similar vein, others blame self-obsessed hyper-consumers trawling the malls, apparently caring not one whit that their waste is burying our planet.

Others see very different bad guys, preferring to blame the irresponsible poor, as in Ronald Reagan's disdain for the "welfare queen" or some people's scorn today for low-income homebuyers who took on mortgages they couldn't handle. For this group, the enemy is anyone who wants government to do "for us" and make us all dependent weaklings.

Others blame radical Islam, pointing to the hostile and violent Al Qaeda as the greatest enemy of freedom and democracy.

Obviously, if the problem is those bad guys, the cure must be getting rid of them. "Our responsibility to history is… to rid the world of evil," declared George W. Bush, just days after 9/11.[11] And we've tried and continue to try, to be sure.

Here at home, too, we strive to lock them away or kill them. In less than two decades, our imprisoned population has grown almost threefold, and we're the only western industrial country that executes people—we killed thirty-seven in 2008, ranking us between North Korea and Pakistan.[12]

The "it's *them*" mindset justifies a take-no-prisoners approach even off the battlefield. "Politics is war conducted by other means. In political warfare you do not fight just to prevail in an argument, but to destroy the enemy's fighting ability.... In political wars, the aggressor usually prevails," wrote David Horowitz in *The Art of Political War*, a pamphlet distributed by Republican Congressman Tom DeLay to colleagues in 2000.[13] Maybe Representative Joe Wilson, who nine years later yelled "You lie!" to President Obama during the State of the Union Address, had read the pamphlet.

Appalled by such ruthlessness and seeking different outcomes, others may nonetheless share at least part of the same basic strategy: Change the players. However it's practiced, the aim of this approach is to replace the bad with the better—with the easy confidence that one can just vote the louts out. We can exchange, for example, a Bush for an Obama and expect "change we can believe in."

### It's our bad nature.

Equally common is quite a different view: While we might say that we ourselves aren't very bad, only they are, in fact a lot of us seem to believe that basic human character is pretty lousy: We're essentially selfish, competitive, and materialistic.

Like a secular version of original sin, we've absorbed Charles Darwin's survival-of-the-fittest as survival-of-the-meanest, not the most adaptive. And this view of our nature long predates Darwin: "*Homo homini lupus* [we are to one another as wolves]," wrote the influential seventeenth-century philosopher Thomas Hobbes.

Repeating a Roman aphorism—long before we'd learned how social wolves really are—he reduced us to cutthroat animals.

And this drumbeat continues. In a 2009 *New York Times* piece all about our cooperative nature, Nicholas Wade concludes with the notion that our good may come from our bad: "The roots of human cooperation may lie in human aggression."[14] Even President Obama began his 2009 Nobel Peace Prize acceptance speech noting that "war, in one form or another, appeared with the first man."

*Private interest...is the only immutable point in the human heart.*

—ALEXIS DE TOCQUEVILLE, *DEMOCRACY IN AMERICA*, 1835[15]

A relative of these diagnoses is put forth by environmental trailblazer Bill McKibben, who's probably done as much as any human being on earth to awaken us to the threat of climate change. He believes that many human beings have gotten a bit too big for our britches. "[T]he idea that everything revolves around us seems to be an obvious feature of advanced cultures," McKibben writes. Centered narrowly on our own species' desires, we've ended up destroying the natural world—ultimately, of course, damaging our own species' chances. So we humans need to "climb down a little bit from the heights on which we have put ourselves," he pleads.[16] It's an important insight.

From this range of assumptions about our aggressive, selfish and presumptuous nature, it's no surprise that many assume the world is as it is because, even if most of us profess to care about others, *those who have a lot, who enjoy being at "the heights," don't really want a world that works for everybody.*

It might mean they would have to give something up, and that's just not going to happen.

## Dead ends

So where do the theories wafting through our cultural ether—"it's *them*" or "it's our nature"—leave us? Not in a very good place.

If today's massive poverty results from qualities inherent in poor people, one hardly knows where to begin—especially since these qualities would appear to be infecting more and more of us. And trying to stamp out all those "evil" ones? It can feel equally futile. Not only do a lot of them apparently live far away in terribly inaccessible caves, but, if badness is at least partly inborn, then new bad ones must be born every minute!

The second set of assumptions about our mean-spiritedness and hubris suggests that, given today's extreme and worsening inequality of access to life's essentials, not to mention to all the extra goodies, there may well be no feasible way to get there from here. There's no way to move toward a fairer, more livable world if those who've got the stuff, and enjoy their dominion over the rest of nature, will continue to scare, bribe, kill, or brainwash the rest of us to protect the—I mean, *their*—status quo.

Either way, we sure seem stuck.

Starting from these assumptions, it *is* hard to imagine solutions. So, across a wide political spectrum many fall back on one remaining hope: the transformation of the human heart.

"To salve the world's wounds demands a response from the heart," writes environmental leader Paul Hawken in *Blessed Unrest*.[17] Rabbi Michael Lerner, another remarkable champion of a better world, calls for his religiously motivated activists' network to pursue a "politics of generosity." Hawken turns to historian Karen Armstrong's description of an earlier time—the Axial Age, 900 to 200 BCE, which gave birth to the world's great religions. He claims that we may be in the midst of a new "spiritual awakening," but we just don't know it yet. Hawken sees the power of transformed hearts in the rise of a myriad of citizen groups. His website celebrates over 100,000, most emerging fairly recent. What will enable them to succeed is their goodness, he suggests. Despite some "clay feet" among civil society activists, he declares his belief in their eventual triumph because their hearts are in the right place, as they share two core values—the sanctity of life and the Golden Rule.

But for eons, sages and saints have been saying that the solution is transforming hearts. Yet despite some astonishingly positive breakthroughs worldwide by important measures, including impoverishment and eco-devastation, we're heading swiftly backward—so swiftly as to threaten life on Earth as we've known it, which makes it kind of hard to find comfort in this cure.

## Rethinking assumptions

What if the most commonly held views of our predicament and its cures can't get us where we want to go, not because they are "wrong" (Who doesn't want more generosity, for example?), but simply because they don't conform to massive and now fast-growing evidence?

It's hard to believe, for example, that the "as-yet-untransformed" human heart—pure and simple—is what's standing in our way when neuroscientists, psychologists and anthropologists, among others, increasingly point to solid evidence of our inborn cooperative and empathetic sides, as well as our need for fairness. I spell these out below. In fact, some scholars convincingly argue, the strength of our pro-social qualities is what distinguishes our species.

These findings pose a challenge to the change-of-heart message: Since virtually all humans have now-proven positive proclivities, why aren't these attributes already showing up more?

That's what I want to know.

Wouldn't common sense suggest focusing first on what gets in the way of our expressing the positives within most of us, before getting too worked up about the need to change ourselves and others?

Equally unsatisfying is the "blaming the few bad guys" frame. It really falls apart once we come to grips with harder-to-swallow evidence that, despite our deeply social nature, most, not a few, of us can be brutal, really evil, in specific circumstances. In this way, it turns out that the "bad human nature"—or "original sin," if you prefer—diagnosis has got it partly right.

The "blaming a few" frame also collapses if we let in the deeper meaning of ecological science. We're learning that from the amoeba to the grizzly bear to the forest deep, we're all inter-connecting and inter-creating. If that's true, the whole notion of one-way force, including one-way blame, is just plain silly.

If we're all connected, we're all implicated.

## DIGGING DEEPER INTO WHY WE'RE IN THIS SCARY PLACE

My hope is to enable us to see that we've been really wrong, and then delight in our error—to delight because we are able to see an eyes-wide-open, realistic pathway forward. This is what "getting a grip" means to me.

Yes, it's tough. But now there is a powerful incentive to step up and face the cold (and warm) facts. Only when we do this work can we each identify meaningful acts we can take now to avert planetary calamity and move toward the world we want.

That's pretty tantalizing.

Imagine not having to stuff one's feelings every day, blocking out the news. Imagine not feeling powerless. Imagine not having to settle for a "random act of sanity" and feeling instead that we are choosing acts, "big" or "small," that really do contribute to turning our planet home toward life because they are accurately aimed at root causes?

Let's begin at the beginning to see whether we can grasp the roots—starting with "Who *are* we, anyway?"

> *So far as I am aware, we [Westerners] are the only society on earth that thinks of itself as having risen from savagery, identified with a ruthless nature. Everyone else believes they are descended from gods.*
>
> —MARSHALL SAHLINS, BIOLOGIST[18]

As noted, the tooth-and-claw version of our early tribal existence still has its grip on us. While Darwin's theory of evolution was a huge knowledge breakthrough, it also muddled our minds. For, if we imagine ourselves to be modern-day apes, just a lot smarter, it's hard to be encouraged. In 1835, well before *Origin of Species*, when Queen Victoria visited the London Zoo to see the apes for the first time, she was appalled. To her, they looked "frightful, and painfully and disagreeably human."[19]

Well, Your Highness, fear not.

"[O]ur line of apes is in a class by itself," concludes anthropologist Sarah Blaffer Hrdy.[20] From what we now know about humans, we could not have evolved in a straight line from the forebears of today's apes, she argues. Genetically, we're just as close to the more tolerant, gregarious and sharing bonobos, according to Hrdy, and the evidence leads her to believe that "as long as a million and a half years ago, the African ancestors of *Homo sapiens* were already emotionally very different from the ancestors of any other extant ape…"[21]

So our roots, Hrdy posits, must lie with a line of primates who brought up their offspring quite differently than do today's Great Apes. From this line, we became distinctly "cooperative breeders"—a far cry from other primates who don't trust others to care for their young. Among hunter-gatherers, it is dads, siblings, aunties, grandmas, and friends who help care for babies from birth, Hrdy reports. Among the Efe in Central Africa, babies enjoy attention from an average of fourteen caretakers in the first days of life; and as they grow, someone other than the lactating mom holds an Efe baby for 60 percent of daylight hours.[22] Hrdy notes that "shared suckling is not observed among wild apes but occurs at least occasionally in 87 percent of typical foraging societies."[23]

In societies where moms have many helpers, they can "devote energy to producing more and bigger babies." And their children have the "luxury of growing up slowly, building stronger bodies, better immune systems, and in some cases bigger brains…"[24] In cooperating to rear our babies, we gained a "combination of empathy and mind reading," without which "we would not have evolved to be human at all," writes Hrdy.[25]

In a word, we can thank our helpless, demanding babies for our distinctly cooperative nature, which made possible a whole lot else—including civilization itself.

Reinforcing Hrdy's thesis is evidence that "for over 90 percent of our existence as human beings we lived, almost exclusively, in highly egalitarian societies," note U.K. professors Richard Wilkinson and Kate Pickett.[26] This is true, they stress, despite the "modern impression" that inequality in human societies has been permanent and universal. Among anthropologists there is broad consensus that humans are unique in our "pervasive sharing" of food, "especially among unrelated individuals," writes Michael Gurven, a leading authority on transfers among hunter-gatherers living as our early forebears did.[27] Except in times of extreme privation, when some eat, all eat. And the most productive hunters share the most.[28]

Hrdy notes that, almost everywhere, hunter-gatherers prefer egalitarian sharing because they grasp that "status striving and self-aggrandizing" can be divisive and therefore dangerous. They go to "great lengths" to "forestall ruptures" that might split the group on which all depend.[29] Of course, we didn't lose this practical preference for cohesion back on the Savannah. Today, most of us recognize and try to nurture connections we can rely on in good times and bad.

> *[Man] is sensible...that his own interest is connected with the prosperity of society, and that the happiness, perhaps the preservation of his existence, depends upon its preservation.*
>
> —ADAM SMITH, *THE THEORY OF MORAL SENTIMENTS*, 1790[30]

From these deep roots, certain natural proclivities stand out.

## THE "GOODNESS"?

**First, we're empathetic cooperators.** As just noted, notwithstanding Darwin's misconstrued notions about competition for survival, it turns out that cooperation explains our evolutionary success just as much. Darwin surmised that primal people judged what was good or bad "solely as they obviously affect the welfare of the tribe."[31]

Cooperation flows in part from hard-wired—or at least "soft-wired"—tendencies, such as empathy. I prefer the term "soft-wired," suggesting proclivities rather than absolutes, given all we now know about the power of context to shape our behavior.

Soft-wired empathy is increasingly well documented. "Brain imaging studies reveal," writes psychologist Daniel Goleman, "that when we answer the question, 'How are you feeling?' we activate much of the same neural circuitry that lights up when we ask, 'How is she feeling?' The brain acts almost identically when we sense our own feelings and those of another."[32]

Babies cry at the sound of other babies crying, Goleman also notes, but rarely at a recording of their own cries. And there's certainly no reason to think we humans might be less empathetic than rhesus monkeys, who've been shown in an experiment to forego food (in one case up to twelve days) to protect another monkey from electric shock.[33]

And here's a discovery that invariably gets at least a chuckle from audiences: Neuroscientists using MRI scans discovered that when human beings cooperate, the same parts of our brains light up that are aroused when we eat chocolate! They note what even a moment's reflection tells us: Cooperation is pleasurable.[34]

In fact, the more we learn about our brains, the harder it gets to talk about helper and helped, giver and receiver, at all. Newly discovered "mirror neurons" in our brains suggest that in some ways we ourselves experience what we observe as if we were performing the action.[35] Hmm. If I give something to another, I'm also experiencing the fun of receiving?

And, there's new evidence that *giving* offers the greater pleasure. In one study, when two groups were each handed a chunk of money, one group told to spend it on themselves, the other to buy a gift, it was the givers who ended up being happier.[36]

Our cooperative nature has really practical implications.

Because we are so adept at sensing what others feel and think, we're uniquely able to create toward a common end—what developmental psychologist Michael Tomasello calls "shared intentionality."[37] Whether it's Social Security or traffic lights or the Sistine Chapel, none is the product of a single person's brilliance but that of numerous people cooperating toward a shared end. (*The Sistine Chapel*? Wait a minute! Haven't we all imagined Michelangelo, the lone genius balancing solo on that high scaffolding? Well, no. Thirteen people helped out, for Michelangelo was an entrepreneur collaboratively making art bearing his name.)

**Second, a sense of fairness lives within most of us.** We have learned that injustice destroys community on which our own survival depends. More than two hundred years ago, even the supposed godfather of greed, Adam Smith, grasped this truth. Of all the social virtues, Smith wrote, we are "in some peculiar manner tied, bound, and obliged to the observation of justice."[38] Today, researchers are finding that even capuchin monkeys demonstrate a measurable sense of fairness.[39]

In fact, so committed are we to the principle of fairness that we will accept less for ourselves if that's what it takes to keep things fair. In a simple experiment, psychologists make subjects choose between the chance of getting nothing for themselves and the chance of getting less than a fair shake. It turns out that at least half of us will walk away with nothing before letting the other guy get away with treating us unfairly.[40]

**Third, we're problem solvers.** Just think about it: Could humans really have made it to almost seven billion if we were really just spectators, shoppers and whiners? We are doers. We are problem solvers who enjoy seeing the impact of our work. The impulse is so great, wrote twentieth-century social philosopher Erich Fromm, that he revised seventeenth-century René Descartes' thought-focused notion of self. Fromm sums us up this way: "I am, because I effect."[41]

**Finally, we're creatures of meaning.** More than simply being doers, we want our doings to have significance way beyond ensuring our own survival. Fromm called it simply the human need to "make a dent" in the wider world. It makes sense, then, that when we act on our deepest values for causes we hold dear, we're measurably happier. In an intriguing experiment, psychologists Tim Kasser and Malte Klar compared students involved in CampusActivism.org with a random group and found that 30 percent of the engaged group were psychologically "flourishing." And the others? Only about 18 percent.

Could it be that the active students felt better even before becoming involved?

The two psychologists probed the question by asking groups of students to write letters to their schools' food service. Some were told to focus only on their personal likes and dislikes, others to write about the ethical aspects of the school's food—such as whether the coffee served was "fair trade." Afterward, the group that had taken an ethical stand recorded a greater sense of "vitality."[42]

We humans have long met our need for transcendent meaning through religion, but also by striving to be good ancestors, ensuring our children's and their children's futures. So, to me, it feels only natural that we'd want to quench part of our deeply rooted thirst for meaning by contributing to the rescue of our threatened planet and, along the way, enhance qualities deep inside us—empathy, leadership, and courage—that this journey brings forth, *if we can just see the way.*

## AND OUR NOT-SO-LOVELY POTENTIAL?

But let's not get *too* pumped about ourselves.

For most of us can be cruel, really cruel. And let me be clear, I'm not talking about the capacity of a tiny minority of us; I mean the vast majority. The Holocaust doesn't prove what a crazed dictator and some sadistic guards will do. Actually, it proves the depravity most normal people will exhibit, given certain conditions.

I know it's touchy. Just the word "evil" makes me squirm a little. After all, I was that little girl in Texas who as a preschooler came home from my friend's Sunday school asking my parents, "What does 'hellfire and brimstone' mean?" They quickly decided it meant they should found a Unitarian Church, and in that church I don't recall ever hearing the word "evil."

But I want to get used to it.

To bring home this unhappy truth about our dark potential, British historian Christopher Browning has a tale to tell. As late as March 1942, he reports, the vast majority—75 to 80 percent—of all victims of the Holocaust were still alive, but "a mere eleven months later" most were dead.[43]

These murders happened, Browning says, because "ordinary" people became killers. He tells, for example, of Reserve Battalion 101: about five hundred men from Hamburg, Germany, many of whom were middle-aged reservists drafted in the fall of 1939.[44]

From working and lower middle classes, these men with no military police experience were sent to Poland on a bloody mission—the total extermination of Jews in Poland's many remote hamlets.[45]

Within four months, they had shot to death, at point-blank range, at least thirty-eight thousand Jews and deported another forty-five thousand to the concentration camp at Treblinka.[46]

"Though almost all of them—at least initially—were horrified and disgusted," Browning writes that over time social modeling processes took their toll, as did guilt-induced persuasion by buddies who did the killing. By the end, up to 90 percent of the men in Battalion 101 were involved in the shootings.[47]

I first learned about Battalion 101 from Philip Zimbardo. You might recognize the name. Zimbardo is the professor who organized the infamous "prison experiment" at Stanford in 1971. He put young people who'd "tested normal" into a mock prison setting where they were divided into prisoners and guards, dressed for their roles, and told the experiment would last two weeks.

But on the sixth day, Zimbardo abruptly halted the experiment. He had to. Using some techniques eerily similar to those in Abu Ghraib prison over three decades later, the "guards" had begun brutalizing their "prisoners," causing severe emotional breakdown. Professor Zimbardo has since acknowledged that one reason he stopped the experiment was that his girlfriend told him he himself had begun behaving like a warden—"more concerned," as he put it, "about the security of 'my prison' than the needs of the young men entrusted to my care…"[48]

Since the beginning of the twentieth century, humans have killed roughly forty million other humans not in war, as we normally define it, but in massive assaults on civilians, from the fifteen million lost in the Russian Gulag to over five million in the Congo. Whether we're talking about a psychologist's carefully designed experiment or genocide in Darfur, the inescapable proof is in: Decent people do evil things under the "right conditions." Pretty horrifying.

*The "right" conditions?*

So, from this grand—and, well, not-so-grand—sweep of human history as well as from lab experiments we've carried out on ourselves, what can we now identify as the conditions fairly certain to bring forth the worst in us?

Three come easily to mind.

> *Power in the hands of a few*: concentrated, unaccountable decision making. At the extreme are slavery and imprisonment. But inequalities in power, which bring out the worst in us, show up in corporate oligopolies, as well as in governments beholden to private interests and one-sided family dynamics that end up in abuse. Because extreme power inequality is implicated in creating the two dicey conditions below—anonymity and scapegoating—it seems to me the most critical condition almost certain to elicit the worst. Interestingly, those associated with "the Left" often focus their outrage on the concentration of economic power, as in massive corporate bureaucracies; whereas those associated with "the Right" most

distrust concentrated, unaccountable government power. Imagine combining our legitimate fears to take on both!

*Anonymity*: social arrangements in which we can be darn well sure we won't be held accountable. Or even caught. Think Ku Klux Klan, with frightening white hoods hiding their identities. Think Vice President Dick Cheney and Big Oil executives in the White House in 2001, discussing energy policy while blithely telling American citizens it was none of our business who was there or what went on.[49] Or, think U.S. financial industry today: "Certainly people in the industry knew that this [financial bubble] was not going to last," notes MIT economist Simon Johnson, but they lived by "a little industry code": IBGYBG. "I'll be gone. You'll be gone." In other words, I'm just an anonymous player. I know when it all implodes, I can slip away unseen. And most did.

Long supply chains involving nameless, faceless—yet very human—"factors of production" also create a type of anonymity that makes it hard for innate empathy to kick in. Few shoppers trying on the three-dollar shirt in Kansas City can connect their hearts with the Cambodian garment worker paid 33 cents an hour, her real wages sinking during the last decade, over eleven thousand miles away.[50]

*Scapegoating*: a culture of blame I've already touched on in which we're each encouraged to see "them" as solely responsible. As with anonymity, scapegoating helps us avoid accountability. Worse, we force those we target to pay a heavy price. Think of the most mundane, bullying on the playground, to the most horrific and vast—genocide.

Once we know what "does us in"—at least these three conditions—we have a real chance to grasp what's needed for us to thrive: We can flip these three negatives, for their opposites seem pretty likely to bring out the best in us, as this book will soon explore. We can also see that these negative conditions share one subtext: *fear*. All three help to create and stoke fear, which itself can induce us to betray ourselves. That's why in Chapters 8 and 9 I explore fear, asking how we can work *with* it in this historical moment.

## STANDING UP FOR OURSELVES

But to make sense of our predicament and our potential today we must first dig deeper still.

For how can we explain the existence in contemporary humans of deeply carved pro-social proclivities, such as cooperation and a sense of fairness, unless we also evolved other capacities? First and foremost, we must have acquired over a very long time enough guts to enforce norms of fairness and sharing, including the stomach to punish, when necessary, those who violated them.

And, indeed, anthropologists tell us that we evolved pretty clear practices, called "counter-dominance strategies," for standing up to those who tried to push us around. Because these strategies protected and fostered cooperation, the success of our species depended on them. And today I'd go so far as to say our very survival depends on them.

One 2006 study in *Science* concludes that when we share standards and some of us "have the moral courage to sanction others, informally," the society "manages very successfully." So notes senior author Bettina Rockenbach in the *New York Times* coverage of her work. Groups "with few rules attract many exploitative people who quickly undermine cooperation," says the *Times* piece. "By contrast, communities that allow punishment, and in which power is distributed equally, are more likely to draw people who, even at their own cost, are willing to stand up to miscreants."[51]

*An avidity to punish is always dangerous to liberty.*

—TOM PAINE, *DISSERTATIONS ON FIRST PRINCIPLES OF GOVERNMENT*, 1795

But it sure seems that in many cultures we humans have lost our touch when it comes to counter-dominance strategies.

*Where did that skill go?*

Yes, it's true, we finally did get beyond feudalism, overthrew legalized slavery, and in democracies women finally achieved the right to vote. But de facto slavery, in the form of human trafficking and forced labor, is on the rise.[52]

And here in the United States, we tolerate a concentration of economic power in which the top 1 percent of households, about a million families, control as much wealth as 95 percent of households put together.[53] At the same time, almost 60 percent of Americans will live in poverty for at least a year during some point in their adult lives.[54]

What happened? What happened to the art of keeping hoarders, power mongers and bullies in check? "'Egalitarian' feels like a fairy tale," a University of Florida student said to me recently.

No one is sure, so I will venture what seems likely to me. My answer begins with our brains.

## BIG MIND, BIG PROBLEM...OR NOT?

As we evolved, our brains got bigger, and our thinking more complex. Our big, complex brains were allowed to evolve, as noted earlier, in part because of the uniquely human phenomenon of "cooperative breeding," anthropologist Sarah Blaffer Hrdy posits. Hunter-gatherer infants, compared to other animals, were nurtured by many adults, not just their parents; such help from cooperating, trusting adults allowed us more time in and out of the womb to grow big brains. These expanding brains enabled many good things that we consider the stamp of our humanity.

But here's the big irony.

These same big, glorious, imaginative brains, made possible by cooperation, also set us up to be vulnerable to what could rob us of the essential preconditions of cooperation.

Sound mysterious?

Not really. Our big, complex brains mean that more than any other species we are creatures of the mind. And minds can create mischief. Humans see reality through frames of meaning that we create, so there is no unfiltered reality for us. We see what we expect to see and literally cannot see what is outside our frame.

I experienced a trivial example of this human quality as I was preparing for Thanksgiving. I searched high and low in every cupboard and closet for our Dutch oven so I could start baking the root vegetables. Frustrated, I finally gave up. Much later, I turned around and there it was—only it held a plant! Because my baking dish had been reframed as plant holder, I was blind to it.

My transient kitchen "blindness" reflects an aspect of humanness that extends all the way to how we see and therefore shape our entire world. That's my claim. The cultures we create flow from the ideas, or frames, we hold that define our reality. These are the mostly unconsciousness assumptions that determine not only what we can or cannot see but also what we believe human nature to be and therefore what we believe to be possible.

We evolved to live so under the influence of framing ideas that they can even trump instinct.

That we are creatures of the mind is just fine, of course, so long as our life-shaping ideas are positively aligned with our nature and thus serve life. But, social philosopher Erich Fromm warns, they aren't always. To stir us to realize the danger within this unique aspect of our humanness—our filtering through socially determined frames—Fromm came up with this mind-bending declaration: "It is man's humanity that makes him so inhuman."[55]

This is what I called the great irony: Our big brains, *made possible by cooperation*, then enable us to create big ideas through which we interpret reality, and these ideas can very well *destroy cooperation.* Just as our big, framing ideas can bring out the best, they can also bring out the worst.

And over the millennia we've fallen for some humdingers—like the idea that kings are born with a "divine right" to order us peons to hand over our precious crops to them. It took us a long time to shake that one! Or, today the idea of "honor" in some cultures that convinces a parent to kill an offspring. And remember the idea that appalled poor Queen Victoria—that we are just vile apes in clothes. Or what about this whopper, put forth with special gusto in the U.S. for over three decades—that the market is "magic," that it works on its own and is infallible.

My point is that we humans can be both disgustingly brutal and beautifully cooperative and empathetic. In large measure, it is our ideas about ourselves that determine the rules and norms we create and enforce, which then elicit our slimy or splendid selves.

And here's the problem: In this do-or-die moment several of our biggest ideas, our mental frames determining what we believe ourselves to be and how communities work, are betraying us, even the very best parts of us.

Yet we now have solid evidence that our species has the inner resources to make the turn toward life.

## WHEN A TREE FALLS

Since this book's first edition, we've moved from catastrophic losses and chronic crises under George W. Bush to another set of catastrophic losses and chronic crisis under Barack Obama.

In less than two years, the world's financial implosion zapped fifty trillion dollars of global paper "wealth"—enough to purchase adequate food for every human on earth for a year. In these years, the number of hungry people in the world climbed by over one hundred and fifty million to reach the greatest number in history. (During the 1990s, an increase of even ten million was seen as a worrisome setback.) And in the U.S., one in every eight homeowners lost, or is on the verge of losing, a home, while experts warn we are only halfway through the pain.[56]

When a big storm topples a big tree, one can often see its roots for the first time; and we are being slammed with a global storm unlike any in my lifetime. What a perfect time to pull back, to get the big picture, and to ask, "Just how did we get here? And what new pathways can we now create?"

As you now know, I believe the answer starts in our heads. Can our already big minds get still bigger, big enough to see the mischief they themselves can do? Can we choose mental frames that enable us to perceive our frames themselves? That's what I'm aiming for. Since humans create the world according to the ideas we hold, if we want a different world, we need some different ideas.

> *[E]ach person has the biological power to interrupt detrimental, derogatory beliefs and generate new ideas. These new ideas, in turn, can alter the neural circuitry that governs how we behave and what we believe.*
>
> —ANDREW NEWBERG, M.D., AUTHOR, *WHY WE BELIEVE WHAT WE BELIEVE*[57]

Sometimes a rude shock is just what's needed to loosen the grip of a dominant but failing idea, allowing us the freedom to choose new ways of seeing.

Imagine poor Alan Greenspan, once the revered head of the U.S. Federal Reserve with the nickname "Oracle," who in 2009 declared himself in a state of "shocked disbelief."[58] His "resolute faith," said the *New York Times*, "that those participating in financial markets would act responsibly" had cracked.[59] I could almost see his big horn-rimmed glasses shattering, for apparently Greenspan had long held the idea that we humans are who we are, independent of context.

Does he now grasp the critical lesson of this crisis—that we respond powerfully to the rules and norms we as a society set, rules and norms that themselves reflect our core assumptions about our nature?

In this moment, our biggest challenge is to let go of the futile attempt to eliminate the bad guys and drop the notion that saving ourselves requires a massive transformation of the human heart. It is to face the discomfort of letting go of failing ideas and discover the exhilaration of exploring new ways of seeing.

It is to recognize that maybe we're already good enough, so our future depends on "fortified backbones"—on developing the courage to stand up for the best within us, a theme to which I return in Chapters 8 through 10.

In other words, maybe we don't have to be better than ourselves, but *truer to ourselves*—truer to all we know…the good, the bad, and the ugly.

# 2 WHERE DID OUR POWER GO?

*[T]he liberty of a democracy is not safe if the people tolerate the growth of private power to the point where it becomes stronger than their democratic state itself. That, in its essence, is fascism....*

—FRANKLIN DELANO ROOSEVELT, 1938[60]

Gradually—it's taken a while—I've come to see the real crisis facing us today is not climate chaos or millions dying of hunger. I say this because solutions are largely known, and big advances are being made daily.

Take food. There's more than enough for us all, and that's counting only the "leftovers"—what's left over after feeding more than a third of the world's grain and fish catch, and most of our soy, to nonhuman creatures who shrink its capacity big-time before it gets to us.[61] Plus, we now know that we could replace chemical, planet-heating, polluting agriculture with ecologically attuned farming worldwide and end up with *more* food—and healthier food, to boot.[62]

We also know there is no scarcity of energy sources that do not heat our planet. Each day, the sun provides us with a dose of energy 15,000 times greater than we're now using in mostly planet-heating fuel. Effective strategies for aligning with this potential are expanding faster than we can say "photovoltaics."

So, that's how I can say that our real problem is not a heating planet or rampant malnutrition. Since, for the most part, we know the answers, and since we now realize that humans come equipped with the inner capacities needed to care about and create solutions, we only have one real problem: our own feelings of powerlessness to manifest the solutions already in front of our noses.

So let's focus with laser precision on a single question: *What's robbing us of power?*

## THE SPIRAL OF POWERLESSNESS

As you now know, my argument is that, in this critical moment for planet home, several prevailing ideas mislead us about our own nature. These ideas also disconnect us from nature itself, as I explore in my 2010 book *Liberation Ecology*. They therefore disempower us.

Opening the front flap of this book, you'll find what I see as a *Spiral of Powerlessness*. It is the scary, self-reinforcing current of some of these limiting beliefs and their consequences.

At its center, triggering our downward slide, is a single premise: lack. There just isn't enough of anything—neither enough "goods" to meet our needs in the world nor enough "goodness" inside us to enable us to create something better.

Whether it is jobs, food, energy (or Zhu Zhu Pet Hamster toys for 2009 holiday shoppers), there is never enough to go around. That's the self-reinforcing premise of scarcity. (Ever notice how close are the words "scarce" and "scare"?)

From there the spiral's momentum quickens.

Believing we evolved in a competitive scramble over scarce stuff, it follows that the modern-day human who triumphed must be, once the fluff is peeled away, selfish, competitive, and materialistic. (Or, at least, that's all we can count on.)

And if we swallow this assumption of a "scarcity of goodness" a caricature of our complexity, of course we can't believe that it's possible to come together in common problem solving. You know...democracy? Assuming a selfish-only human nature, we're sure someone would always muck it up. Even the possibility of a "common good" becomes a pipedream.

If we're incapable of deliberating to make choices together, we'd better—quick—find a mechanism we can't mess up that can sort things out *for us*. That's where what Reagan called "the magic of the market" comes to the rescue. Best turn over our fate as much as possible to it—after all, it's driven by the one thing we know is reliable, self-interest. Best keep "government" out.

Making government the enemy really means making us the enemy of ourselves. It becomes easy to forget that government is nothing more than what we decide to do together. This forgetting can be disturbingly humorous: In 2009, 39 percent of Americans agreed that "the government should stay out of Medicare."[63]

Because Americans love Medicare, of course, many assume it couldn't have anything to do with the government they've been taught to disdain.

Degraded in the public's mind and increasingly driven by private interests, government ends up being less and less capable. A special assistant to President Reagan made the agenda clear in 1987, stating, "We shouldn't want a proficient public sector."[64]

And citizens feel the change. In 1964, three quarters of Americans said they trusted government to do the right thing most of the time.[65] Today, less than a quarter feel that way.[66] Fewer people are drawn to public service, and government's resources shrink.

Not to fret, though. If real democracy—that is, deliberating together to shape common purpose and strategies—is suspect, privatize and commoditize all that we can, from health care to prison management to war-making itself, in order to take full advantage of the market's "magic."

But in all this, we've consistently failed to ask what *kind* of market.

Yes, the market, an exchange of goods and services, has been around a really long time. Trading my extra corn for your extra cabbage seemed like a good idea. But over time we've fallen for a peculiar notion: that *any kind* of market can create benign outcomes—even ours, driven by one rule—highest return to existing wealth, those who run the corporation and own its shares. Within this set up, wealth naturally accrues to wealth. In the U.S., that means one family, the Waltons of Wal-Mart, can end up possessing roughly as much wealth as the poorer 40 percent of the American people.[67]

Poverty, insecurity, and fear all increase, confirming the dreary premises about our selfish nature that set this dismal spiral in motion in the first place.

And, as we feel increasingly vulnerable, trust—every society's essential glue—dissolves further. The share of Americans who believe that people can be trusted has dropped from almost half in 1976 to barely one in three thirty years later.[68]

## SPEEDING THE SPIRAL

Sometimes, I've learned, the ideas shaping our view of the world seep into our consciousness over very long stretches of time. Sometimes, though, ideas take hold really fast. Much depends on the willful intention and dedicated resources of those propagating them; and over the past thirty years, we've found out just how effective this combination be.

An early drumbeat sounded, many scholars note, in a 1971 rallying-the-troops memo by Supreme Court Justice Lewis F. Powell. Sternly he warned the U.S. Chamber of Commerce that any alternative to the unfettered (what I prefer to call "one-rule") market meant "bureaucratic regulation of individual freedom—ranging from that under moderate socialism to the iron heel of the leftist or rightist dictatorship."[69]

He singled out Ralph Nader as particularly menacing, though at the time all young Ralph had done was save us from exploding Corvairs.[70]

Powell's alarm was heard. It spawned comprehensive action to convince Americans that any measure to keep in check vast accumulations of wealth, or any policy to ensure wide access to the market—from the minimum wage and capital gains taxes to inheritance taxes and anti-monopoly action—is not only counterproductive but virtually immoral.

Foundations supported by large corporations and wealthy individuals, wanting to convince Americans that a one-rule economy is good for us, poured $1 billion into their tax-exempt think tanks and media campaigns in the 1990s.[71] Plus, over $35 million a year has gone into spreading the message on college campuses through, for example, student newspapers, and tens of millions more have bolstered academic programs grounded in this worldview.[72] Overall, says David Brock, a former insider among defenders of concentrating power, those spreading this point of view spend $300 million a year to win the "war of ideas."[73]

Little wonder that so many have come to see government as something done to us or for us by taking "our money." So, of course, the less of it the better.

And the premise of "lack" continues its self-fulfilling spin: As our problems, from educational failure to climate change, worsen, the presumption that our fellow humans are fundamentally lacking in compassion seems to be proven before our eyes. So trust erodes still further. Gun sales go up; and in one year alone, 2009, the number of formal neighborhood-watch groups jumped by 40 percent.[74]

## ELECTIONS PLUS A MARKET...THAT'S DEMOCRACY?

What this downward spin tells me is that we've ended up with a condition that linguists call "hypocognition," the lack of a critical concept we need to thrive.

And it's no trivial gap!

What's missing is a workable, effective concept of democracy itself. Swept into this vortex of powerlessness, we can't imagine democracy in which we citizens have power—democracy vital and compelling enough to create the world we want. In fact, given the assumptions driving the *Spiral of Powerlessness*, it's no mystery why most Americans grow up absorbing the notion that democracy boils down to just two things—elected government plus a market economy.

Since in the United States we have both, there isn't much for us to do except show up at the polls and shop. I like to call the stripped-down duo—elections plus a market—Thin Democracy, because it is feeble. (Thanks go to my mentor, political philosopher Benjamin Barber, for this fine term.) I've tried to capture its essence in *Idea 1* on page 59. Please take a moment to ponder it, reflecting on what jibes with your experience and what does not.

We breathe in this definition like invisible ether, so it's easy to jump over an unpleasant fact: Real democracy accountable to citizens and our peculiar variant of a market economy are based on opposing principles. The word "democracy" derives from the Greek: demos (people) plus kratos (rule). Thus democracy depends on a broad dispersion of power allowing each citizen both a vote and a voice. But our particular variety of a market economy, driven by highest return to shareholders and corporate chiefs, moves inexorably in the opposite direction. By continually returning wealth to wealth, a one-rule economy leads to an ever-increasing concentration of power.

## LIZZIE'S LESSONS

In the early 1900s, Lizzie Magie tried to warn us. Lizzie was a concerned Quaker, worried that one-rule capitalism would do us in. So she came up with a board game she hoped would entertain us but also serve as an object lesson: It may take all night, but the rules of the game eventually drive property into the hands of one player and the fun's over for everybody.

Well, Lizzie's idea got into the hands of Parker Brothers. They called it Monopoly, and the rest, as they say, is history—history that, in this case, reveals exactly what dear Lizzie was trying to tell us about one-rule economics. Just five companies sell well over half of all the toys in America.[75] More generally, in 1955, sales of the top five hundred corporations equaled one-third of the U.S. gross domestic product. They now account for two thirds.[76]

As corporate wealth concentrates, so does private wealth: After two decades of income growth among the wealthiest, from 2002 to the start of the Great Recession in 2007, two thirds of all income growth in America went to the top 1 percent of families.[77] This massive upward transfer of wealth meant that by 2007 the top

10 percent captured a bigger share—half—than at any time since record keeping began in 1917.[78]

Within the one-rule economy of Thin Democracy, even advances in productivity—more output per worker—don't benefit workers. In early 2009, when worker productivity rose to its highest level since 2003, corporations used the gain to strengthen profits and labor's piece of the pie shrank faster than it had in nine years.[79]

So, no surprise: The gap separating the average U.S. CEO's compensation and the average U.S. worker's pay has widened *tenfold* in one generation, enabling the CEO to earn as much by lunchtime on the first day of the year as a minimum-wage worker earns the entire year.[80]

We shouldn't be shocked (but I still am) that income inequality in the U.S. is more extreme than in India or Bangladesh.[81] We've reached the point that the combined wealth of the four hundred richest Americans, $1.27 trillion, is roughly comparable to the total annual income of half the world's people.[82]

I find it fascinating that those defending Thin Democracy wail that redistribution of wealth is unfair and socialist, yet seem blind to, or even celebrate, this massive upward redistribution we are experiencing.

But what to call this disaster for our planet? My struggle to find a term ended recently, thanks to Citigroup.

Citigroup?

Yes, in an October 2005 report, "Plutonomy: Buying Luxury, Explaining Global Imbalance," we're told that *plutonomy*—an economy driven by and for the rich—is "here, and going to get stronger." So clients should keep "riding the gravy train" and invest in "toys for the wealthy." In a plutonomy there's no such thing as a "U.S. consumer," we learn; there are only "rich consumers" and "the rest, the 'non-rich,'" who account for "surprisingly small bites of the national pie."[83]

I envy Citigroup's clear prose.

So, since we didn't learn from Lizzie, we've arrived at plutonomy. We failed to catch on; to keep the game going, we citizens have to devise rules to ensure that wealth continually circulates. Otherwise, it all ends up in one player's pile (in my household, usually my brother's) and the rest of can't even afford a house on Baltic Avenue.

Yet under the spell of one-rule economics, for decades many economists and business leaders have ignored this truth, as well as new jaw-dropping evidence that markets, even fast-growing ones, don't by themselves create livable societies: Worldwide, during the 1990s, every one hundred dollars in economic growth reduced the poverty of the world's billion poorest people by just *sixty pennies*.[84] And in the next decade the global financial crisis so spread poverty that by decade's end more than one in every seven people on earth goes hungry.[85]

Denial runs so deep, though, that the pro-corporate British journal, *The Economist*, apparently with a straight face, can describe inequality deepening worldwide as a "snag" in the system.[86] And well-meaning academics, with Columbia University's Jeffrey Sachs in the lead, can rally us to end global poverty by exporting our assumed-to-be successful economic model to them.[87]

Most remain blind to Thin Democracy's pitfalls.

## THIN DEMOCRACY'S DANGERS

### Death to open markets

A one-rule economy's ongoing concentration of economic power ends up destroying exactly what we Americans love about a market—that it's open, competitive, and trustworthy.

First off, as Citigroup knows, wealth naturally accrues to wealth in a market economy, unless rules guiding its continual circulation are in place (lesson number one of Monopoly).

So, with public oversight systematically stripped away, the financial sector had swollen by the early 2000s to reap 40 percent of corporate profits.[88] And concentration has sped far beyond this one sector. In the world's grain trade, two companies control roughly three-fourths of the market; one, Monsanto, accounts for 88 percent of the area planted worldwide with genetically modified seed and/or seed with biotech traits. Six corporations control most global media, from publishing to movies, five account for almost two thirds of U.S. gasoline sales, and four out of five of the chips in the world's PC's come from just one corporation, Intel.[89]

No market so tightly controlled can fairly be called "free."

Centralized power doesn't just block the entry of competitors. As I note below, such tight market power also translates into political power, used—among other bad things—to deny buyers the information every economist tells us is essential to keeping a market healthy.

One stark example? For years, almost nine out of ten Americans polled have said they want to know if a food has been genetically modified—a disclosure that is required in thirty-seven countries (even totalitarian China). But Monsanto and other makers of genetically modified seeds have succeeded in denying this information to Americans.[90]

Perhaps most disconcerting of all, such concentrated economic power means we citizens are easily held hostage. Throughout 2009, how many times did we hear the term "too big to fail" applied to globalized financial institutions? And when pundits completed the sentence, we got the message: Either we bail out the behemoths or face economic Armageddon. What a choice. Thin Democracy takes us there: Citizens end up in the hellish position of "choosing" between dependence on unaccountable, non-transparent financial bodies or economic ruin.

As the new decade opens, Congress is still debating financial regulation reforms, but none so far seem likely to come to grips with this underlying too-big-to-fail threat.[91]

To bury that threat requires breaking up monopoly power, but the already-way-too-big get bigger faster: From the 2007 beginning of the Great Recession to 2009, the three largest U.S. banks acquired ten top rivals, increased their market share, and grew their combined assets by an average of almost two thirds.[92]

All this suggests that the relationship between the market and government isn't what we've been led to believe. It could be the opposite: According to market gospel, the two are mortal enemies, when actually government and the market are fast friends.

Competitive, fair markets can't be sustained, it turns out, without a genuinely democratic polity setting fair rules to keep them open.

So, just as with the protection of civil liberties, open markets depend on *us*; they depend on citizens who support fair rules and their enforcement to keep them that way. Understandably, corporations want the opposite; they seek control over markets to ensure highest returns—not because they're run by bad people, but because the rules we've set up encourage them to act that way.

History bears out this truth. It shows us, too, that there's no reason it has to remain this way.

When American citizens and officials have stepped up to the plate, a lot has improved with remarkable speed, particularly in the period from 1933 to 1945. During that time, Americans created fairness rules—including the right of workers to organize, Social Security, and a legal minimum wage—that enabled our country to begin dramatically narrowing the gap between most of us and a tiny minority at the top.[93]

From the 1940s to the 1970s, all income groups advanced, but the poorest fifth gained the most—more than doubling their real family incomes.[94] As a result, broad-based economic prosperity continued for decades: Median family income grew four times faster between 1947 and 1973 than it has since, as America has forsaken Lizzie's commonsense insight.[95]

Unfortunately, Thin Democracy's pitfalls don't stop here.

## Warping of politics

Concentrated economic power, flowing from a one-rule economy, ends up warping political decision making, wrecking the very tool we need to address all our biggest challenges. In 2008 lobbyists spent $3.3 *billion*—twice their spending a decade earlier—pushing their private agendas.[96] And, with the 2010 Supreme Court's overturning of restrictions on corporate political advertising, corporations' potential to overwhelm citizens' voices multiplies. More than two dozen lobbyists already walk the corridors of power in Washington for every one person we citizens have elected to represent our interests there.[97]

To understand for whom all these lobbyists work, consider that corporate chiefs and boards of directors want to make money; and it is tough, year after year, to corner market share and keep coming up with clever new products.

Isn't there a more surefire way?

MIT economist Simon Johnson assures us there is. Corporations "think [the way] they can best make money is to shape the regulatory rules" of government to their favor, he observes. Financial corporations "washed away…regulatory rules around everything…that kept the financial sector under control."

In their work to bend government, corporations are "doing their job," Simon stresses.[98] But they can succeed in making it their "job" only because we citizens haven't been doing ours: protecting democracy itself. When lobbyists grossly outnumber citizens' representatives, private power supersedes public power, and we arrive at what might best be called "privately held government."

*Government by organized money is just as dangerous as Government by organized mob.*

– FRANKLIN DELANO ROOSEVELT, MADISON SQUARE GARDEN, 1936[??]

It's exactly what FDR warned us about seventy years ago.

Here are just four frightening examples showing why privately held government works against us:

- **The financial system.** With our country still suffering from the worst economic collapse since the Great Depression, Wall Street in 2009 spent $334 million lobbying to block new rules to prevent the risk taking and deception that brought on the crisis.[99] So far these efforts have prevented key reforms, including allowing states to create their own tougher rules.[100] And as of early 2010, Wall Street is set to pay itself nearly $150 billion in compensation and bonuses—that's enough to solve the year's budget crises of all fifty states.[101] Banks "are still the most powerful lobby on Capitol Hill," said Illinois Senator Dick Durbin in 2009. "[T]hey frankly own the place."[102]
- **Our health.** In 2009, U.S. health-care companies spent $1.5 million each day lobbying Congress to block real reform; meanwhile, forty-five thousand Americans die unnecessarily every year due to lack of health insurance, according to Harvard Medical School research.[103] And our infant survival rate ranks forty-fourth among nations, barely better than that of Croatia, according to the CIA.[104] In 2009, when health-care reform finally looked to be on the verge of passing, health

insurance corporations' stocks soared, no doubt in part because they'd been able to block efficiency measures and competition from a public insurance option.[105]

- **Food safety.** Though five thousand Americans die each year from food-borne illnesses, the food industry lobby is able to block mandatory food recalls and adequate food safety inspections, which were cut almost in half between 2003 and 2006.[106]
- **Work safety.** More Americans die—fifty to sixty thousand a year—from work-related illnesses or toxic exposure than die from breast cancer and prostate cancer combined, according to the National Institute of Occupational Safety and Health. Yet industry has so effectively resisted workplace safety inspection that today the federal agency in charge has fewer inspectors than in 1975.[107]

No wonder more and more Americans feel their democracy has been stolen—and they know by whom. By 2002, almost 90 percent of us agreed that corporations have too much influence in Washington. This common sense insight by citizens didn't stop a majority of the Supreme Court, chosen by presidents steeped in a Thin Democracy worldview, from allowing unlimited spending by corporations to sway elections, as mentioned above. But even with this anti-democracy ruling, citizens have pathways to reclaim the political process, as I explore in Chapters 5 and 10.[108]

More than unworkable, Thin Democracy is dangerous. The above examples of the power it gives a tiny minority to put its gain ahead of our common well-being reflect only one danger. Here are four more.

### The fragility of centralized power

Contrary to lessons drummed into us, concentrated power is often not resilient, efficient, or smart. The Incas and the Aztecs, huge civilizations, fell to conquistadors in no time, while the leaderless, decentralized Apaches fended off harsh attacks for two centuries.[109] Concentrated power often isolates itself and thus fails to learn. Think only of the "I'm the decider" bunker stance of the Bush White House that led the U.S. into a trillion-dollar war in Iraq based on faulty intelligence. Or consider how fragile the highly centralized global financial empire turned out to be, as fifty trillion dollars—$8,000 per person on earth—in market value went "poof" in a single year.[110]

### Missing problem solvers

The flipside is that the centralized power of Thin Democracy leaves most of us feeling powerless, robbing the planet of just the problem solvers we most need. It encourages us to look to the "market" or CEOs or government higher-ups for answers, but our planet's problems are too complex, pervasive, and interconnected to be addressed only from the top down. Solutions depend on the insights, experience, and ingenuity of those people most affected—all thwarted when citizens are cut out and manipulated, and when decisions get made, often secretly, by the few.

Put slightly differently, solutions require in-the-moment inventiveness and widespread behavior changes, and both depend on the engagement and "buy-in" of citizens. So Thin Democracy undermines precisely the broad-based commitment our world so desperately needs.

## Mal-aligned with our nature

Thin Democracy can't create healthy societies because it is mal-aligned both with human nature, as Chapter 1 explored, and with the wider laws of nature, as I explore in my 2010 book *Liberation Ecology*. Thin Democracy denies our rich complexity, *so it fails to tap the best in us and also fails to protect us from the worst.*

By "best" I mean our innate needs and capacities to *connect and affect*: to live in communities of basic trust and to feel a sense of agency (power!). Most literature about what makes people happy ignores our need for power; yet a sense of control over our lives is essential not only to mental but physical well-being.

Thin Democracy's extreme inequalities, not only in reward and in status, but also in our sense of agency, kills us...literally: A long-term study of U.K. civil servants in the 1960s found that men working in low-status jobs with little power, such as doorkeepers and messengers, suffered death rates three times higher than administrators of the highest grade. Differences in risk factors such as smoking or obesity could explain only a third of this huge discrepancy.[111]

It turns out that inequality itself is bad for us, all of us. Presumably because we evolved in egalitarian societies, we don't "do inequality" well in modern societies. The greater the inequality, Professors Wilkinson and Pickett document, the more severe are the society's social and health problems—and not just for the lower classes, but across the whole society. On their graph tracking the correlation of inequality and dysfunction in twenty-one countries, the United States is the outlier: Both our inequality and our social and health problems are so severe as to put us in a sad class by ourselves.[112]

Denying a sense of agency to so many, offering scarce opportunity to feel involved in decision making and connected to something grander than our own survival, with stark inequalities violating our innate sense of fairness—Thin Democracy is bound to fuel paralyzing despair and alienation.

*And the "worst" in us?*

How does Thin Democracy take into account our capacity for cruelty and callousness that lives not in a few but in most of us, under the right (i.e., wrong) conditions?[113]

Some defenders of Thin Democracy's "let the market decide" premise see their stance as based in a hard-nosed assessment of humans and accuse critics of naiveté. Strange, then, that Thin Democracy actually fails to register our negative potential. By reducing democracy to elections plus a one-rule market, it creates the very conditions proven to bring out the worse—most critical among them, extreme power imbalances.

From this perspective, Thin Democracy defender and former Fed chair Alan Greenspan suddenly seems like the naïve one. Apparently he couldn't see the economic collapse coming, even as alarms blared, because his frame didn't include the negative human behavior causing it: No rational person, he believed, would take risks that might damage one's "reputation," since it has "significant economic value." Greenspan's mentor Ayn Rand called this motivation "rational selfishness."

But Greenspan's model misses the obvious: Reputation is a social construction; and for it to serve society's well-being there must be *transparency* so that our actions are known by others. Plus, of course, for concern about reputation to check ruthlessness requires rules and norms aligning a good reputation with a lot more than just ending up with the biggest "take."

Ironically, Greenspan oversaw the dismantling of *precisely those rules and norms* within the financial industry that might have aligned reputation with positive outcomes for society.

Seems his frame blinded him.

## Failure to bring meaning

Finally, Thin Democracy is dangerously vulnerable because its demeaning premises can't satisfy our higher selves' yearning for transcendent meaning.

Many U.S. soldiers now risk their lives in war, believing they're serving a high calling. But the built-in logic of one-rule economics mocks their idealism. Since 9/11, thousands of American soldiers have made the ultimate sacrifice in Iraq and Afghanistan, while executives of U.S. armament corporations have made a killing, doubling their own compensation.[114]

At the same time, Thin Democracy's materialism and concentrated wealth help to swell the numbers of people who feel alienated, humiliated, and angry. These feelings open some hearts to extremist, violent ideologies—both religious and secular—that claim high moral ground and offer adherents everlasting glory. Such extremism can appeal not only to the world's poorest but also to some among the well-off.

Americans were in shock in late 2009 when five educated young men from solid Northern Virginia families were arrested in Pakistan at the home of a man linked to a radical jihadist group banned by the Pakistani government.[115] And those arrests followed news that young Somalis from Minnesota had been recruited for terrorism—one even blew himself up in Somalia.[116]

Young men have long seemed most susceptible to violent ideologies, but a sixty-five-year-old in Gaza told the British *Observer*, "I know at least twenty of us [elder women] who want to put on the [suicide bomber's] belt." They've "found a use for themselves," she said.[117] How deep runs our need to feel useful, a need unmet for so many people in today's world.

Ultimately, Thin Democracy's demeaning premise can't hold a candle to the fanatics' uplifting, absolutist visions—right or left.

In all, Thin Democracy gives democracy itself a bad name. Its profound shortcomings help to explain why many countries' initial enthusiasm for it is now waning. Between 2000 and 2005, in ten African countries, polls showed citizens' preference for democracy falling—in Tanzania by almost half. In 2000, two thirds of Latin Americans polled said they were dissatisfied with democracy.[118] Chile, thought to be among the more successful Latin American democracies, saw the percentage of young people voting fall to 9 percent in 2009.[119]

## THIN DEMOCRACY, THE VICTOR? NOT REALLY.

In writing this new edition, an intriguing paradox hit me.

On the one hand, no one can deny that Thin Democracy has taken hold with historic swiftness: Once "government as enemy, market as savior" claimed the nation's psyche in the early 1980s, our society began a U-turn.

Real wages in the United States, having grown in every decade since 1830, abruptly stopped growing in the 1970s.[120] And then came the unraveling of the rules and norms—from financial industry oversight to protection of workers' rights—that had been moving us toward a "middle class" society of fair opportunity. In the process, the media became just another fast-consolidating industry helping to instill in us the Thin Democracy frame: Today, 91 percent of radio talk shows are vehemently anti-government voices scaring us with talk of "death panels" and threats of "government takeovers."[121]

Thin Democracy appears to have us in its grip and many Americans feel robbed of power. And yet…and yet, most of us appear not to have been robbed of core insights that put a lie to Thin Democracy's assumptions. For example, 2009 polls report that:[122]

- **Government Responsibility.** Six in ten Americans believe that "government should do more to promote the common good," with almost three quarters believing that "government regulations are necessary to keep businesses in check and protect workers and consumers;"

- **Security and freedom.** Well over half believe that "freedom requires economic opportunity and minimum measures of security, such as food, housing, medical care and old age protection and almost two thirds believe that government "should guarantee affordable health coverage for every American;"
- **Inequality and fairness.** Almost two thirds believe "the gap between rich and poor should be reduced, even if it means higher taxes for the wealthy;"
- **Climate change.** Two thirds believe "America must play a leading role in addressing climate change…complying with international agreements on global warming."

Americans may "diss" government, as Thin Democracy driven by narrow interests makes it dysfunctional. Yet to me these findings reflect an allegiance to fairness and an appreciation that one's own well being is linked to the "preservation" of society, as Adam Smith astutely put it.

This basic human wisdom, perhaps soft-wired in us over eons, doesn't seem to have been erased even by the well-orchestrated and well-resourced march of Thin Democracy. But what will it take for citizens to trust that wisdom and to find our power to create a more life-serving frame?

For one, as we take in the meaning of today's scientific breakthroughs about the nature of life itself—its quality of interconnectedness and never-ending, co-created change—we can sense motion. Instead of feeling stuck, we can see today's tragic detour as exactly that. Awareness that reality is never static can encourage us to try on a new kind of humility.

With all our fancy forecasting—from ten-day weather reports to the Fed's inflation predictions—we can be lulled into presuming that we can see into the future pretty well. Thin Democracy can feel solidly in place. But actually, we can't, and it isn't. History doesn't unfold in neat, even increments. It moves in messy, surprising jolts, and in this unprecedented era, the surprises could even intensify.

And here's the big upside: Recognizing that in this unique moment it's not possible to know what's possible...we discover we are free. We're free to throw ourselves into the most thrilling, planetary struggle our species has ever known. We can *intentionally* evolve more life-serving mental maps. We can probe deeply, asking together: What might be a more complex understanding of ourselves and a richer understanding of democracy—both strong and vital enough to meet today's challenges, and compelling enough to stand up to extremists' claims?

It starts with seeing possibility.

# 3 NEW EYES

*Hope remains only in the most difficult task of all:*
*to reconsider everything from the ground up,*
*so as to shape a living society inside a dying society.*

—ALBERT CAMUS (1946)[123]

Human beings don't walk into a meaning void. That's not who we are. So if we are to let go of the mental map that is generating Thin Democracy—and deepening global crisis—more is needed than simply acknowledging its frightening pitfalls.

We must have at least a glimmer of what can replace it. And that's not easy, for some of the West's most influential opinion shapers carry the presumption of scarcity right down to ideology itself. Referring to corporate capitalism, *New York Times* columnist Thomas Friedman declared, "I don't think there will be an alternative ideology this time around. There are none."[124]

Neither can we suddenly invent out of whole cloth something as profound as a new way of seeing the world. So the great news is that, as democracy reduced to elections plus a one-rule economy is increasingly failing, a richer form is taking shape. By its nature, though, it's not as easy to describe as Thin Democracy.

It is, nonetheless, real.

Yet because of the way human brains work, we probably won't be able to recognize it unless we first believe it's possible. Contrary to the "seeing is believing" cliché, in fact *believing is seeing*. We have to believe something is possible before we can see it; so my goal is to enable us to believe a new, stronger concept of democracy is emerging. We can then recognize its pioneers, and from there, realize our own power to act. We humans are social mimics, after all. We take our cues from one another.

In other words, I want to help us see what is happening all around us but still invisible to most of us.

I know the challenge well because I was one of the blind ones not long ago, as I began asking what a workable democracy might look like. I figured I'd follow a few leads on engaged, more participatory forms of problem solving and write a book about what I learned. I expected to turn up relatively slim pickings—a dozen or so examples. In the end, my real headache was having to choose among hundreds of breakthroughs to write *The Quickening of America*. I still laugh when I recall, on my author's tour, a *U.S. News & World Report* interviewer confessing, "I went to Harvard, and I had never heard about any of what's in your book!"

That book led to several more, requiring me to venture far and wide with my "new eyes." The experiences changed me forever. They've given me a new lens through which I can now see what I like to call Living Democracy—democracy as a way of life, no longer something done to us or for us but a way of living together that we shape ourselves.

It is *citizens engaged in the continuous generation and dispersion of problem-solving power.*

It's new, and it's really old.

## THE PATH

Australian historian John Keane, among many, sees democracy as fairly new, invented in the eastern Mediterranean not too long before the birth of Christ. It "implied something revolutionary," he writes. "[T]he whole idea that flesh-and-blood mortals could organize themselves as equals,...to decide on this or that course of action, was a sensational invention."[125]

Not really. The more we learn about prehistory, the more we realize that, while of course "representative democracy" is a fairly modern invention designed to meet the needs of complex societies, "the whole idea that flesh-and-blood mortals could organize themselves as equals" is really old. It is how humans have lived for most of our time on earth.

Living Democracy furthers a long historical strain expressed throughout our history and in many indigenous practices the world over. Benjamin Franklin, for example, drew on the Iroquois Confederacy's philosophy, which, for hundreds of years before one Pilgrim set foot here, had succeeded by practicing inclusive decision making that valued diversity.[126] For his part, Thomas Jefferson understood democracy as citizens' everyday participation in public power.

> *[a]ctive liberty, the principle of participatory self-government, was a primary force shaping the system of government that... [our constitution] creates.*
>
> —SUPREME COURT JUSTICE STEPHEN BREYER[127]

Building on this long strain in human history, Living Democracy that I see emerging is not merely a formal government setup—elected bodies and countervailing centers of power. It is embedded in a wide range of human relationships. So—and here's the vital part—its values and practices apply just as much in economic life or cultural life as in political life. We don't have to leave our humanity behind when, for instance, we enter the workplace.

Put very practically, Living Democracy means infusing the power of citizens' voices and values into every part of our public lives and removing the highly concentrated power of money from governance.

Rest assured, Living Democracy isn't a new, fixed "ism," blueprint, or utopian end-state. It continually evolves, incorporating new experience as more and more people reject the view that democracy is a set system and begin to work with the idea that democracy is a set of system qualities, *driven by core human values.*

Chapter 1 contrasts assumptions behind the dominant and failing Thin Democracy with those motivating a richer practice of democracy, one that could become democracy's next historical stage.

So here's a question for you: As you skim *Idea 1: Thin Democracy vs. Living Democracy* on the following page, does Living Democracy strike you as naïve or utopian, even if you don't want it to? If so, perhaps your reaction reflects assumptions about human nature itself.

## IDEA 1: Thin Democracy vs. Living Democracy

| THIN DEMOCRACY | LIVING DEMOCRACY |
|---|---|
| **What is it** | |
| Democracy is a set system: elected government plus a market economy. We may have to keep cleaning it up around the edges, but our democracy is basically complete—it's the culmination of human history. | Living Democracy is a set of system-qualities that shape daily life. Its values of inclusion, fairness, and mutual accountability infuse not only political life but economic and cultural life as well. Living Democracy is always evolving; it's never finished. |
| **How does it work** | |
| The free market, along with government and corporate executives and experts, determines what happens. Citizens vote, work, and shop. A single rule—highest return to shareholders—drives the market, which does tend to concentrate wealth and power...and then influence the political process. But there's no other way; tampering with the market would kill its efficiencies and our way of life. | Citizens use their voices and values to shape public choices. They set rules to keep wealth continually circulating and to keep its influence out of politics. They decide what is a market commodity and what is a right of citizenship because it is essential to life. Moving beyond a one-rule economy (highest return to existing wealth), "values boundaries" guide the market, from environmental protections to anti-monopoly laws. Citizens' conscious shopping choices also foster healthy communities. |
| **Who gets involved** | |
| Only officials and celebrities have public lives. | All citizens have public lives. As buyers, savers, investors, voters, advocates, students, employers, workers, and members of social benefit organizations, our actions create the quality of our communities and the wider world. |

| What's required for effectiveness | |
|---|---|
| Public life is ugly and alienating. No special learning is needed, just thick skins and big egos! (Plus access to big bucks.) | Democracy is learned, and we practice its arts—active listening, creative conflict, negotiation, mediation, mentoring and other relational skills—we reap the joy of effectiveness. |
| **What motivates people to engage?** | |
| Self-defense. Getting involved in public affairs is a necessary hassle to defend our private lives and interests. It is the burden a free people must bear to earn our liberties. | We humans know our own well-being depends on healthy communities and that only in public engagement can we fulfill our need to connect with others in common purpose, to make a difference, to express our values and to fully respect ourselves. Engagement is part of the good life. |

In addition to the common assumptions about ourselves I touched on in Chapter 1, a lot of Americans assume human beings aren't up to the engagement in the world that Living Democracy implies. Most people just want to be left alone, we're told. In fact, George W. Bush's ally Grover Norquist named his anti-tax movement the Leave Us Alone Coalition.

But the withdrawal of Americans into our private worlds, which many scholars have documented, reflects our culture, not our nature. We increasingly withdraw for a reason, I believe. We feel overpowered, not empowered. If we reflect on our evolution within socially connected tribes and compare the vast differences in voting and civic engagement across countries and communities, we can put to rest the fear that Living Democracy is beyond us.

## OF MEANS AND ENDS

So the way forward seems clear. We start, as I've suggested, by dropping the distracting debate over whether we humans are essentially good or bad. We're then free to identify and work together to eliminate triggers proven to bring out the worst in us while deliberately building on those that bring out our best, including our clearly life-affirming proclivities: to be cooperative, to be fair, to be effective, and to search for meaning.

They make possible a very different way of thinking about democracy.

It is no longer primarily a tool, an instrument for making better decisions—something we do to further some deeper principle, like justice. For as long as democracy is viewed mainly as a tool to get what we want, it can easily be ditched when it's not convenient. As when, on Election Day 2002 New Hampshire GOP organizer James Tobin paid (and was later convicted) for massively jamming get-out-the-vote phone lines in the state's Democratic Party headquarters. As in 2003, when the Bush White House chose to retaliate against its political enemy Joe Wilson by illegally "outing" his wife Valerie Plame as a CIA agent, endangering lives. As when some Americans chose in August 2009, to kill honest debate on health insurance reform by hurling invectives and shouting down opponents in what became "town hall" tirades.

Living Democracy is shorthand, in part, for fair play and decision making through honest dialogue that includes the voices of all affected. As such it is not a convenience; it is essential to human flourishing. It is our how our species incorporates lessons along the human journey.

Why is Living Democracy worthy of embrace as an intrinsic value?

Because it dissolves the three deadly conditions shown again and again to bring out the worst in humanity. Stated positively, it creates the conditions we now know are essential both to human thriving and the flourishing of our beleaguered planet:

- In place of centralized power, Living Democracy works for continuous dispersion of power.
- In place of anonymity, Living Democracy builds communities of transparency and trust.
- In place of scapegoating—the blame game—Living Democracy promotes a mutuality in which we hold ourselves accountable, not just the other guy.

## AN ECOLOGY OF DEMOCRACY: FIVE QUALITIES

Living Democracy, possible because of this richly complex nature of ours, isn't a set system. Above I described it instead as a set of system qualities. It's critical that we begin to name them, for human beings have a tough time creating what we have no words to describe.

Here, then, is my stab at five qualities I see transforming democracy into a lived practice able to solve problems that have long seemed insurmountable.

## 1 Dynamic, never finished

Between our nation's founding and 2006, our fifty states have ratified over six thousand state constitutional amendments.[128] Living Democracy's dynamism means it isn't limited to redressing singular injustices; it's able to create ever more inclusive, fair, and effective ways of making decisions. A "learning democracy" might be another apt moniker to describe what is emerging, for it's always a work in progress to which each new generation applies the lessons of its experience.

> *Democracy is a process, not a static condition....*
> *It can be easily lost, but is never fully won.*
>
> —JUDGE WILLIAM HASTIE[129]

One recent "sighting" of this dynamism is "participatory budgeting," a newly emerging form of citizen deliberation over key public choices. It began in Brazil, where the wealthy have long held a tight grip on how city funds are allotted. To break that grip, in 1990 members of Brazil's Workers' Party—now one of the country's largest—came up with participatory budgeting, a process in which as much as a fifth of a city's budget gets allocated through multistep, face-to-face neighborhood deliberations.[130]

In the birthplace of citizen budgeting, the southern Brazilian city of Porto Alegre, some one hundred thousand citizens have so far taken part. As a result, the share of resources going to poorer neighborhoods and to programs benefiting the poor has grown.

Another dividend? The noticeable decline in corruption under the watchful eyes of so many citizens. Visiting a neighborhood near Porto Alegre in 2003, I admired the big, new community center and heard about a new school and clinic.

Asking, "But how can you afford all this?" I was told by smiling locals that less corruption meant more funds for the community. In other words, the new participatory system means greater government efficiency: In 1988, an administrative dollar in Porto Alegre brought three dollars in services; ten years later it brought seven dollars' worth.[131]

Participatory budgeting has spread to hundreds of Brazilian municipalities, and their experience has inspired citizens in fifteen other countries to try it, from Durban, South Africa, to Saint-Denis, France.[132] In 2010 an Australia MP in the district of Heathcote is inviting citizens to decide through the Internet how best to allocate approximately $300,000 to support local infrastructure and jobs. Via video, the legislator explains the context and asks citizens to rank eligible proposals already drawn up by local community organizations.[133]

And here at home, in a handful of cities—Portland, Oregon; Seattle, Washington; Birmingham, Alabama; Dayton, Ohio; and Saint Paul, Minnesota—citizen councils afford citizens direct say over significant public money and priority setting.

Living Democracy's dynamism—its unending evolution—can also be glimpsed in the new, citizen-initiated, legally binding "community benefit agreements" you'll read about in the following chapter.

### 2 Values-guided, not dogma-driven

Just mentioning the word "values" unnerves many Americans; they believe we're hopelessly divided, so best not to go there. In truth, we're hope*fully* united on some essential policies reflecting deeply shared values. Chapter 2 concluded with quite a list, revealing significant common ground, from views on climate change to economic security.

If we're surprised, it's because the media visibility given to extremist ideology distorts its presence in our culture.

Overexposure of hard-line tactics and intimidation is itself a symptom of Thin Democracy, which has enabled highly consolidated media, allowing it to profit from sensationalism that is disconnected from the weight of actual public opinion. Americans who, for example, dismiss health care reform out of hand and fear that President Obama has a "secret agenda" to bankrupt the country, are not even close to a majority of us: They comprise slightly less than one fifth of voters, according to 2009 research.[134]

Among the remaining 80 percent, it seems likely that there is common ground to be developed, reflecting values that fuel the dynamism of effective democracy: fairness, inclusion, and mutual accountability. By "mutual accountability," I mean simply all sides shouldering responsibility—the opposite of the blame game. It is recognition that just pointing fingers at those up there—the president, wealthy CEOs—and bemoaning our victimhood leads nowhere.

Jack Shipley, a part-time rancher in his sixties living near Grants Pass, Oregon, helped teach me this lesson. Jack has long been a leader in the Applegate Partnership, entrusted by the state with watershed protection planning for an eight-hundred-square-mile chunk of southern Oregon.

"The environmentalists criticize us for talking to loggers," Jack told me a few years ago. "But how can we find solutions if we don't include all people who are part of the problem?" he asks. So members of Jack's group, the Applegate Partnership, began wearing a signature button around town: one word with the familiar diagonal "no" slash through it. The word is "They."

If there is no "they" to blame, we realize all sides need to act. And the Applegate Partnership did, arriving at a plan all could accept.

Another example of mutual accountability in action that brings to life the values of fairness and inclusion began in south Texas in 1990. Jolted by the closing of a Levi Strauss plant that left one thousand people jobless, two San Antonio church-based groups began searching for ways to ease the plight of the unemployed and of poor workers.

Communities Organized for Public Service (COPS)—which now reaches fifty thousand families through twenty-seven parishes—and its sister organization, Metro Alliance, were upset. They saw new, well-paying jobs being created, but San Antonio's many low-skill job seekers, many of them Hispanic, weren't filling them. Yes, the citizen groups could easily have jumped on the big companies, calling them racist for not hiring locals. Instead, they decided to be problem solvers: They identified the real stumbling block as the lack of effective job training.

Then the two organizations' members—homemakers, bus drivers, ministers—formed a committee to come up with a solution themselves. The fruit of their labor is QUEST—Quality Employment Through Skills Training—that now boasts over three thousand graduates who are prepared not just for any job but for skilled, well-paying ones. More than a year after graduating, 91 percent of QUEST participants had jobs with an average hourly wage several times higher than in the minimum-wage jobs many had held.[135] Four other cities have replicated QUEST's model and together have trained fifty-five hundred people.

Driven by widely shared values, not fixed dogma, Living Democracy evolves as citizens bring those values to public engagement.

## 3 Learned, not automatic

Humans are innately social beings, it's true, but that doesn't mean we're necessarily born knowing how to "do democracy" effectively. More and more people worldwide are coming to understand democracy not as something we simply inherit and defend but as a learned art. Democratic skills, they are saying, can and must be deliberately taught—and practiced—just as are reading or cooking or dribbling a basketball.

Of course, if we're not good at these things, they're not much fun. Running after tennis balls for hours, I've learned, gets pretty tedious. But as we gain skills, including those of "doing democracy," our lives become ever more rewarding. (An introduction to these "arts" is our booklet *Doing Democracy: 10 Practical Arts*, downloadable at smallplanet.org.)

Young people are among those leading the way.

In the spring of 2007 at the University of California Santa Cruz, I met with students who had created their own strikingly successful course, the Education for Sustainable Living Program. Now in its seventh year, it has spread to seven California campuses. Over two hundred eager students enroll annually in Santa Cruz and over six hundred statewide; as of 2009, approximately four thousand students have participated.

"We could never have gotten this course off the ground," an initiator Aurora Winslade told me, "if the eight students who started it hadn't committed to studying communication skills together and using them with each other." The students worked hard to incorporate teachings called Nonviolent Communication, developed by Marshall Rosenberg. The approach centers on honestly expressing observations, feelings, and needs, as well as learning to let go of judging that too often wrecks communication. Aurora also praised help from the *Facilitator's Guide to Participatory Decision Making*, found at communityatwork.com, and the training offered there.

What I see, and love, is that these young people are taking the arts of democracy as seriously as any of their big, external goals. And it is working.

Eva Stevens, one of the program's 2009-2010 organizers at Santa Cruz involved in the course during all four undergraduate years there, told me it was "one of the hardest, but most rewarding experiences that I've ever had. I felt I created the change I want to see."

Now thirty, Aurora, picked by the university to be its Sustainability Manager, sees the value from a bigger perspective. She is struck, she said, by how "advanced young activists, both in Santa Cruz and nationally, are in their ability to work in groups and hold effective meetings." When they begin to pursue campus sustainability with older, more experienced staff, administrators, and faculty, "frequently they're frustrated and surprised" at the contrast. She continued: "Communication skills that students gain in groups like the Education for Sustainable Living Program—listening, most importantly, and reflecting back what is heard, along with planning and facilitating meetings—benefit them as much as or more than any other single thing learned in college."

"They serve us in work, personal life, and civic engagement, but," she added, "they are rarely taught outright, especially in higher education."

But that can change.

Chapter 6 suggests that schools, businesses, community institutions, and elected bodies are effectively learning democratic arts such as *active listening* and addressing conflict through *negotiation* and *mediation*, as well as *mentoring* and *reflecting on experience*.

### 4 Power-creating and power-sharing, not controlling

So much of political talk obsesses over who's got power and who's losing it—as if there were only so much to go around. (One more instance of the scarcity presumption?) Yet, taken to its Latin root, *posse*, power means "to be able;" it is simply our capacity to act. So maybe we should be talking less about power's division and more about its creation—what's really needed to solve our problems.

Living democracy's practices expand power by enabling more people to act on their values and interests. In other words, Living Democracy widens the circle of problem solvers. It expands problem-solving power because it taps into the experience and insight of people closest to the problem. It thrives on the creativity engendered when diverse perspectives meet, as well as the commitment to action that people willingly make when they "own" and are a valued part of the plan. In the story of QUEST above, San Antonio's corporations gained ground because citizens stepped up to remove a barrier to their finding qualified job candidates. Everyone gained.

In a successful struggle to decentralize school decision making in Hammond, Indiana, participant Patrick O'Rourke captured this notion of expanding power, noting that the new setup "broadens the base of decision making in a way that empowers everyone... [B]uilding administrators don't lose out if teachers are more creative...they win. Everyone wins."[136]

Chapter 5 explores the notion of generative, relational power.

## IDEA 2: We All Have Public Lives

YOU

**EDUCATION**
- student
- educator
- parent
- taxpayer
- voter / policy maker
- volunteer

**RELIGIOUS LIFE**
- participant / congregant
- leader
- contributor / supporter

**MEDIA**
- viewer/reader
- opinion giver
- creator: blogs, websites
- volunteer/ supporter (e.g., community radio)

**CULTURAL, RECREATIONAL, AND VOLUNTARY ORGANIZATIONS**
- consumer / patron
- organizer / participant
- member
- supporter
- leader
- advocate
- volunteer
- contributor
- teammate

**CIVIC LIFE**
- financial contributor
- service recipient (e.g., police, courts)
- policy shaper through civic organizations and political parties
- taxpayer
- voter
- volunteer
- advocate

**HUMAN AND HEALTH CARE SERVICES**
- client
- patient
- recipient
- consumer
- member (e.g., voluntary association, self-help group, community, clinic, etc.)
- voter and policy shaper

**ECONOMIC LIFE**
- consumer
- worker
- employer
- saver / investor
- owner
- voter / policy shaper
- rate payer (e.g., utilities)
- member (e.g., union, chamber, interest group)
- professional associates

## 5 Everywhere, not isolated

In Living Democracy, it's possible to align our inner selves. We don't have to chop ourselves in pieces and leave some of the best of us at home as we venture into our public lives.

What a boon to sanity.

Living democracy's values of fairness, inclusion, and mutual accountability "work" throughout the many dimensions of our lives. In political life, for example, it starts with removing the power of concentrated wealth and creating avenues even beyond voting for citizens' views to be developed and heard. But it doesn't stop there.

Notice that I'm using "public life" to refer not just to what officials have but to all the roles we play—including voter, buyer, employer, investor, saver, worker, and volunteer, as *Idea 2* suggests. Living Democracy's values apply in diverse settings, from politics and economics to education, policing, the media, and more, as the next chapter sketches. This is what I mean by "everywhere."

But trickiest to grasp is democracy emerging in economic life, so I'll dwell here a moment.

The ecological worldview in which Living Democracy is emerging enables us to see ourselves not as isolated atoms but as nodes in networks of relationships. Corporations then become just one channel we create to organize relationship networks. This means that corporations are *neither independent of us nor unchangeable monoliths*. A lot shifts: We wake up to our own power, the multitude of ways in which we already *do* shape corporations and *can* redirect them to life-serving ends.

With this view of economic life, in Living Democracy businesses respond to market cues, yes, but with accountability standards that citizens set, from tax and trade rules to environmental and buyer-safety protections. We recognize both formal government channels and informal influences—including our own daily choices and organized advocacy—that we can use to keep the market fair and life-promoting.

As Lizzie Magie tried to alert us, we citizens have to take the rule-setting function of economic life seriously, or our society ends up like Monopoly at the end of the evening—the fun's over for everybody because one player gets all the good property and the rest of us are, well, about to join the homeless.

Once seeing the economy as embedded in a culture of democracy, purchasers also use the power of marketplace choices to send ripples calling for healthy and fair producer practices, as in the growing Fair Trade movement I pick up later.

## SPEEDING A SPIRAL OF HOPE IN ACTION

These five qualities of Living Democracy generate a spiral of human growth and satisfaction I've striven to capture in the *Spiral of Empowerment* that you'll find inside the back cover. In place of "lack," the scary premise of the downward spiral inside the front cover, *possibility* is the heart of Living Democracy. It is a confidence that as we come to value our own creative, collaborative soft-wired potential, as well as appreciate nature's laws—learning to live within a self-renewing ecological home—we discover there's more than enough for all to live well.

I first experienced the consequences of replacing the premise of lack with that of possibility as a lightning bolt, when in my twenties I learned that there was more than enough food in the world to make us all chubby…and there still is.

That's when *I learned that we create the scarcity we fear.*

Future generations may well scratch their heads: You mean, in the early twenty-first century the U.S. feedlot system put 16 pounds of grain and soy into cattle to produce only one pound of beef on their plates? You mean that with the amount of water used for that one pound of beef a person could have bathed for months?

I learned that this irrationality took off, even though inefficient and harmful to health, because one-rule economics leaves millions of people too poor to buy food. Their inability to make market demand for food keeps grain so cheap that it's profitable to feed vast amounts to animals.

In other words, the we are creating scarcity of food from plenty.

Similarly, possibility appears once we drop the scarcity lens surrounding energy. To pick but one example, just one fifth of the energy in wind alone would, if converted to electricity, meet the whole world's demands, reports a Stanford-NASA study.[137]

Overall, the U.S. economy remains "astoundingly" wasteful, conclude the authors of *Natural Capitalism*, as "only 6 percent of its vast flows of materials actually end up in products."[138]

Imagine, then, the potential to meet real needs, as we discover our power to shift from staggering waste toward equity and efficiency.

An awareness of possibility itself undermines a focus on raw, self-centered competition, leaving us able to refocus not on the goodness of human nature, which seems to deny human complexity, but on the undeniable goodness in human nature, including the deep positive needs and capacities to connect and affect.

From there, the *Spiral of Empowerment* quickens.

We gain confidence that we can learn to make sound decisions together about the rules that further healthy communities. Then, as we begin to succeed, easing the horrific oppression and conflict that now rob us of life, we reinforce positive expectations about our species.

The destructive mental map loosens its hold. And as these capacities and needs—for fairness, connection, efficacy, and meaning—find avenues for expression, they redound, generating even more creative decision making and outcomes.

In this way, "getting a grip" doesn't mean gritting our teeth and binding ourselves to dreary duty. With this more complete view of our own nature and of what nature offers, it instead becomes an exhilarating adventure.

# 4 WHAT DEMOCRACY FEELS LIKE

*'So this is what democracy must feel like.' I bet I've have heard this twenty different times in completely different settings—it doesn't feel foreign when people experience it but democracy is a need we don't always know we have.*

—MARTHA MCCOY

Martha leads Everyday Democracy, a Connecticut group that's helped tens of thousands of Americans discover a need—*experiencing* democracy—that's so seldom met many of us have forgotten we have it.

Her work tells us a lot about what happens when people remember. In 1999, her center began working in Kansas City with a diverse citizen coalition distressed that high school test scores were sinking and half the students were dropping out. This educational breakdown, they realized, was linked to life in neighborhoods where people felt unsafe, disconnected, and powerless. And they wanted to do something.

So residents from all walks of life—in the end, over thirteen hundred—began meeting in study circles, creating trust and generating solutions to augment a school reform process already underway. Over just eight years, graduation rates rose to 70 percent. Spanish-speaking parents started (and now run) a "homework help line." Public housing residents created a tenants' association and youth sports camp and are helping to rid a neighborhood of ten drug houses. In addition, over one hundred young people, including some school leavers, worked together to clean up the downtown.

Martha and these gutsy Kansans are part of an emergent ecology of democracy in which Americans are discovering what Living Democracy looks, tastes, and sounds like. It's no longer a distant, fixed structure. Democracy "becomes us," they are finding, in both meanings of the phrase. Their actions and parallel initiatives around the planet are helping to shift our focus from democracy as simply a thing we "have"—elections, parties, a market—to democracy as intricate relationships of mutuality that we create daily.

To give you a sense of this new way of seeing (and being) democracy, here are just nine of its many dimensions, along with hints of how they are already changing lives.

## NINE DIMENSIONS: SOME GLIMPSES

### 1 Citizens are reclaiming their political power from the grip of concentrated wealth—a key to the unfolding of the other eight dimensions of Living Democracy.

If there's any gain to be had from the pain of the 2008 financial collapse and "cures" that so far seem to be failing to address its underlying causes, it's this: Americans are angry. For many, the power of corporate America has never been so blatant; and they are busy strategizing the most effective ways to counter the Supreme Court's recent overturn of limits on corporate political spending.

They refuse to settle for "the best democracy money can buy," and their caustic clarity is fanning the fire inside grassroots-led reforms for voluntary public financing of campaigns. It is one practical, proven pathway beyond the big-money, corporate grip on our democracy.

The tool is Clean Elections legislation that enables a candidate—including those of modest means, like a teacher or a waitress—to run for office, and win. Would-be candidates need only raise very small contributions from a certain number of voters to prove their viability. They then qualify for enough in public funds to run a strong race.

For just over a decade in Maine and Arizona, it's been working to purge money from the race for the legislature—so most legislators there no longer feel beholden to their underwriters. In Connecticut, a similar law went into effect in 2008, and already eight in ten legislators have won their seats using public funding. While at this writing Connecticut's law faces a legal challenge, it fortunately comes not from those opposed to the approach but those wanting the law to give third parties a better chance.

In other states certain key races are now "clean," and, in 2010, legislation is pending in both houses of Congress—they're called Fair Elections Now Acts. Americans can put their outrage at corporate lobbying power to good use by supporting these bills.

With Clean Elections, citizens start to trust again. Voter turnout in Arizona has increased by almost half in presidential elections since 2000.[139] At publiccampaign.org, find out about your state.

If you need even more motivation, just tally up the cost of not acting. Each American household is now paying out $1,600 yearly in tax breaks, subsidies, and other welfare for corporations and wealthy special interests—the tip of the iceberg of the true cost of private power over the public purse.[140] Then compare: Just six dollars annually from each of us would cover the costs of all campaigns for national office, calculates a leader in the reform movement YouStreet.org.

An obvious bargain.

To keep all eyes on this prize—truly democratic government—I return to Clean Elections in the final chapter, where you'll meet two of my personal heroes and get a taste of what a clean legislature can accomplish.

## 2 Citizens are striving to make government their tool—a fair-standard setter, a public convener, and more, so government isn't burdened by the much pricier job of damage control.

In Thin Democracy dogma, Big Government is the bugaboo: It steals our money and our privacy. "Government is not the solution to our problem; government *is* the problem," Ronald Reagan warned us in his first inaugural address. Citizens are made to fear that going for what they desire and know is right, like ending poverty and rescuing the environment, would unleash the big, bad state.

So they pull back.

The maddening irony is that those who scare us with the threat of Big Brother government are too often the same people who cut back essential government services and turn them over to private interests....thus *making* government scary.

Living Democracy depends on seeing through this mind twist. It depends on citizens shaping and trusting government as their tool. And that starts with exposing the misleading big-versus-small government frame—it means recognizing that what really matters is whether government is accountable to citizens.

> *Government's job is to set high standards, let the market reach them, and then raise the standards more.*
>
> –THOMAS L. FRIEDMAN, *THE NEW YORK TIMES*[141]

Accountable government, setting fair standards and rules, actually reduces the need for big government to clean up after the damage is done. From this frame, we see the cost of government action to end poverty or rescue our environment with new eyes. The real cost is our government's inaction:

- By 2008, almost 40 million Americans were living in poverty—many more than the entire Canadian population—and that was before the Great Recession took its toll.[142] Set aside, if you can, the incalculable human suffering of poverty and the loss to society of human gifts that poverty leaves undeveloped, and consider some of what we can tally up.

- So many Americans are poor—with one-half of our children dependent on food stamps at some point in their upbringing—that the annual cost to our society is staggering, even counting only lost economic output, higher health care expenditures, and the impact on crime. Spending on incarceration alone, for example, could buy a Harvard education for each of the two million (mostly poor) people locked up.[143]

  The total cost to the U.S. associated with child poverty comes to nearly $500 billion a year.[144] That's almost our entire defense budget!
- Similarly, enforcing standards to protect the environment is a steal compared to the mega-billions needed to deal with the messes once made. One in four of us lives within four miles of one of these messes—officially designated toxic waste sites. "Superfund" cleanups of the hazards have already cost tens of billions of dollars since they began in 1980. And, over the next thirty years, an additional $250 billion may needed for as many as 350,000 such sites, reports the Environmental Protection Agency—some of which will be paid for with our tax dollars and much of the rest passed on to us in higher prices.[145]
- Or think of the cost of government failing to act now to avert the worst climate-change scenarios. It is a mounting bill estimated already to be as high as one fifth of the world's GDP.[146]

Only accountable government can prevent people-killing poverty and environmental degradation. And we know how to make government work for us because we've done it. Remember the 1960s

War on Poverty—naysayers' proof of government ineptitude? Actually, Americans cut the poverty rate in half during that decade.[147]

Doing what it takes to uproot poverty—enforcing anti-monopoly laws, protecting employees' right to organize, maintaining a federal minimum wage that's really a living wage, creating job opportunities, assuring universal health care, guaranteeing quality day care for all children—none of this requires big government, only effective government.

Nor would restoring tax rates aligned with the fairness principle of ability to pay enlarge government.

During the last forty years, average tax rates for the wealthiest one-tenth of one percent of Americans have been cut in half. In at least one recent year, eighty-two top U.S. corporations paid *zero* taxes;[148] and in 2008 America's favorite bail-out beneficiary, Goldman Sachs, paid just .6 percent (the decimal point is no typo) in taxes on its profits.[149]

And for the rest of us? That's another story: The tax rate on the earned income of most middle-class families is now higher than on dividends and capital gains, which mostly benefits the wealthy.[150]

> *The subjects of every state ought to contribute towards the support of the government, as nearly as possible, in proportion to their relative abilities....*
>
> —ADAM SMITH, *THE WEALTH OF NATIONS*, 1776[151]

Moreover, rescuing the environment could start with simply requiring the government to *stop*—stop handing out rewards for its destruction. No big price tag there, just the guts to say no to fossil fuel lobbies. An estimated $700 billion worldwide in subsidies now encourage environmentally devastating practices such as over-pumping groundwater, clear-cutting forests, and burning fossil fuel.[152]

My aim here is simply to underscore that we can free ourselves from the fear-mongering. Consider this finding: A 2007 in-depth examination of poverty and its cures concludes that it would take only $90 billion a year for ten years to cut U.S. poverty in half. Simply letting the Bush administration's tax cuts for households earning over $200,000 expire would more than cover this life-saving turnaround.[153]

And we now have plenty of examples of what can happen when citizens make government their accountable tool, successfully enacting new rules resetting the economic logic that now ensures ecological devastation:

- One is the "producer-responsibility" or "take-back" law I take up in Chapter 10. It requires manufacturers to shoulder responsibility for the recovery and reuse of what they put into the world. It's already working in twenty-one states and over two dozen countries.[154]
- Another commonsense solution to global heating that doesn't enlarge government is "tax shifting." Europeans are beginning to tax "bads," not "goods," to encourage environmental citizenship. Sweden, for example, has lifted on average $1,100 from each household's income tax and shifted it mainly to vehicles and fuel.[155]

In addition to acting as fair-standard setter, government in democracies answerable to citizens can also serve as our efficient financial agent. But how easy it is to get confused here, too! We're told that Social Security, Medicare, and Medicaid are three *entitlement* programs eating up almost half the federal budget. And we think, "Egads, big government is killing us."

Entitlement? Of course we're entitled; we paid. But "big government?" I don't think so.

In two of these programs, government collects and dispenses our money via what's known as the FICA tax of 7.7 percent on gross earnings, which allows us to support each succeeding generation of retiring elders—without which about 40 percent would now be living in poverty. But here's the little-appreciated fact: Medicare's administrative costs are significantly lower than those of large private insurers and HMOs.[156] And for Social Security, administrative costs amount to less than 1 percent of benefits. That's a tiny fraction of what privately managed investment accounts charge.[157]

This is what I mean by government as citizens' "efficient agent." Let's not let the current need to fix Social Security—because, starting in the 80s, presidents have raided its assets to cover tax cuts for the wealthy and more—blind us to its virtues.

Another, most basic, standard-setting task of citizens in Living Democracy is identifying what should not be allocated by the market because it is essential to life and is therefore a right.

- Historically in the U.S. and elsewhere, K-12 education has been a right.

- Most people in industrial societies have also removed health care from the market, saving themselves vast sums while achieving superior health outcomes. The French, for example, enjoy a life expectancy two years longer than we do while spending roughly half as much on health care per person.[158]
- For many, a decent federal minimum wage should also be in the "rights" column; and strong wages don't seem to impede overall economic resiliency. Consider Norway, where workers' average hourly wages are among the world's highest; yet when global recession hit in 2008, its jobless rate was just a third of ours.[159] (Note: If our minimum hourly wage of $7.25 had kept up with CEO compensation over the last thirty years, it would be almost $19!)[160]

Recognizing the threats of global heating and world poverty, more and more people realize that rescuing our planet—and having a functioning market—depends on reclaiming government from private interests. Let's not let the Court's ruling on corporate spending deter us. Let's learn from our compatriots in Maine, Arizona, and Connecticut how to wrest government from money's influence so it can become our tool for creating the world we want.

Finally, a story.

It captures powerfully for me the effectiveness, not costliness, of government in its role as public convener and fair-standard setter. It comes from Brazil.

In 1993, that country's fourth largest city, Belo Horizonte, reframed access to healthy food as a human right, a mind shift setting off enormous ripples. "If you are too poor to afford healthy food, you are still a citizen," Adriana Aranha, a leader in this reframe, told me. "The city is still responsible to you."

A new city food security agency convened business, civic, union, religious, university, and other leaders, who came up with dozens of civic partnerships enabling poor people to get healthy food—ultimately benefitting four in ten of city residents.

Their outside-the-box innovations include fair-price produce stands on city land, supplied by forty local farmers; open-air restaurants serving twelve thousand subsidized meals daily; and city-sponsored radio broadcasts leading shoppers to the lowest-priced essentials. Their ingenuity led to a Green Basket program that links hospitals, restaurants, and other big buyers directly to local, small, organic growers and spurred dozens of community gardens, as well as forty school gardens, to become "live labs" for teaching science and environmental studies.[161]

"We're showing that the state doesn't have to provide everything; it can facilitate. It can create channels for people to find solutions themselves," explained Adriana, now a leader in Brazil's national "Zero Hunger" campaign.

The impact?

In just one decade, these city-coordinated innovations helped reduce deaths among young children by 60 percent. And the number of children hospitalized for malnutrition is now less than a third of what it was when the shift to food as a right of citizenship began.[162]

The cost?

Less than 2 percent of the municipal budget. In other words, for about a penny a day per city resident, thousands more children live.[163]

### 3 Investors, savers, and purchasers are infusing democratic values into their everyday economic choices.

Living Democracy's values, including fairness and mutual accountability, are showing up in an invest-with-social-purpose movement. It took off here in the mid 1990s and already accounts for 11 percent of the roughly $25 trillion in total assets under professional management.[164] Stock purchasers are realizing they can exert positive power not only by deliberately choosing companies that behave in ways more aligned with their values but also by using their stock ownership to speak out on company policy.

Investor pressure on corporations has been credited with impacts ranging from eliminating discrimination based on sexual orientation at the credit company MBNA to eliminating the sale of mercury-containing thermometers at J.C. Penney's.[165] In 2007, a group of McDonald's shareholders backed Florida's farm workers' demands on that company. The SEC supported them as well, and McDonald's gave in.[166]

And as governments beholden to private interests fail to protect labor rights—with the United States and China still unwilling to ratify basic international labor conventions—purchasers and producers are stepping up themselves. They've partnered to create a Fair Trade economy. In it, a certifying body insures that producers receive a fair price and use environmentally sustainable practices. Fair Trade producer cooperatives also receive a premium they can use for such community benefits as a new school.

The certifier attaches a label to Fair Trade products so purchasers who are determined to end poverty can find them. Already, the buying choices of coffee lovers alone are benefitting more than one million poor producers and workers in fifty-eight countries.[167] In the United States, more than thirty-five thousand retail locations carry Fair Trade Certified products, including Target, CostPlus, Starbucks, Costco, and Dunkin' Donuts.[168]

### 4 Citizens are setting values standards, as well as creating new legal tools, that shape the behavior of corporations.

In one sense, living democracy means returning corporations to the role envisioned by our founders: they are instruments to serve society's well-being.

In this light, muscular campaigns by citizens to redirect the behavior of corporate giants are not a separate species of "activism" but a key part of democracy-building. In 1997, Rainforest Action Network showed the way. With a staff of only twenty-five at the time, and a handful of conscientious shareholders, it ratcheted up its challenge to Home Depot for using wood from ancient, largely untouched forests.

Some probably scoffed. Who would have bet that their ingenious efforts (including using Home Depot's own store intercoms to enlighten surprised shoppers!) would within two years convince the company to halt its use of old-growth wood? And that such chutzpah would trigger a cascade among other big wood suppliers wanting to avoid bad publicity?

And I certainly would not have guessed that in 2003, even as Big Tobacco kicked and screamed, two hundred citizens' groups, the World Health Organization, and leaders from forty-six African countries could succeed in birthing the world's first public health treaty: the Global Tobacco Treaty. In effect since 2005, it bars tobacco corporations from advertising or interfering with public policymaking.

By 2009, one hundred sixty nations—but not the United States—had ratified it, making it one of the "most rapidly embraced treaties of all time."[169]

The magnitude of this triumph hit me, though, only when I learned that, if current trends hold, tobacco will kill one *billion* people by century's end.[170]

Another citizen breakthrough, bringing the corporation within the democratic fold to serve the community well being, was born in California almost a decade ago.

In Los Angeles in 2001, the Staples Center sought a $70 million downtown expansion, and twenty-five citizens' groups pulled enough weight to win the nation's first big "community benefits agreement"—not a bunch of feel-good promises but legally binding accords with businesses and local governments guaranteeing that living-wage jobs, affordable housing, and environmental protections would be part of the expansion.

After that sweet 2001 victory, one citizen group set its sights higher: a piece of the $11 billion expansion of the Los Angeles International Airport, around which are "the most densely populated neighborhoods of any airport in the country and among the poorest in L.A.," Madeline Janis told me. She heads the Los Angeles Alliance for a New Economy, a hybrid research-communications-organizing outfit founded in 1993.

"The airport had increasingly horrible consequences for people living there—the worst rates of asthma, and noise so fierce you can't hear yourself speak. So some schools have no windows; they're like fortresses—horrendous.

"When we started, fatalism—'There's nothing we can do'—had set in. It was the 'coalition of the defeated,'" Madeline said. "But groups came together—labor, teachers, parents, neighborhood associations—and we spent a year building trust. People began to feel they could dream, and over ten months, we negotiated among ourselves exactly which seventy priorities we'd ask for. We trained people to be negotiators. And we won—half a billion dollars in community benefits funds.

"It even means moving a whole school," said Madeline, "and millions for job training. It means every single employer that even touches the airport has to go to the community first to fill jobs." The 2005 agreement also includes money to reduce airport noise, emissions, and traffic, and it assures ongoing monitoring of the airport's health impact on residents.

"All this came out of the community, some of it from people who'd never taken on anything beyond demanding a stoplight, if that," Madeline told me excitedly. Citizens trained to be spokespeople, to organize community meetings, and to hold effective press conferences. They found their voices to stand up for their community.

Since then, more than a dozen such Community Benefit Agreements have been achieved in Los Angeles, and more in cities from Pittsburgh to Seattle. But Madeline stressed to me that the Alliance isn't just shooting for more Community Benefit Agreements, project by project. "That's impractical," she said. The goal is a "paradigm shift transforming the way the city does all development."

For Madeline, "it's about democracy, about empowering people." In the new paradigm, "any public investment" must benefit "the community—the people and the planet," she said. And Madeline sees the shift now being built into certain federal initiatives, such as the Obama administration's climate change legislation, where green jobs would be created in the context of community accountability.

Before moving on to the next dimension of Living Democracy, let me break with the positive to make a critical point: This task—citizens setting the values boundaries within which corporations function—has been made significantly harder by an invisible-to-the-general-public shift over the last one hundred fifty years.

Remember that at the corporation's birth in the early 1800s, there was no confusion about who was in charge: the corporation was chartered by local governments to meet particular needs such as building a road or bridge. But beginning in the mid-1800s, with the rise of the influence of railroad titans and other "robber barons," corporations began acquiring for themselves Supreme-Court recognized rights—due process, free speech, equal protection, and more—that enable them to defy the public's will: for example, to block enforceable standards they don't like or to influence the outcome of elections.

> *...constitutional ordinances earned on the field of battle as charters of human liberty, have been turned into the shield of incorporated monopoly.*
>
> –SEYMOUR D. THOMPSON, ADDRESS TO KANSAS BAR ASSOCIATION, 1892[171]

The oxymoron "corporate personhood" evolved to describe this democracy-defeating ascendance of private power.

In response, a citizen movement–including Republicans, Democrats, Libertarians and Progressives–is fighting to reverse the granting of certain constitutional protections to these non-human entities. The Supreme Court's 2010 ruling protecting corporations' power to influence elections will no doubt add steam to the movement.

By 2009, over a hundred U.S. municipalities, mostly in Pennsylvania, were challenging corporate rights. Some have, with the help of the Community Environmental Legal Defense Fund in Chambersburg, Pennsylvania, passed ordinances asserting community rights and banning damaging corporate practices, such as factory farming and the spreading of sewage sludge; and in one township, a first-in-the-nation ban on mining by corporations.[172]

Citizens in the Maine towns of Shapleigh, Newfield, and Wells resisted the mining of their groundwater by Nestle for its Poland

Spring bottled water by officially declaring that within their boundaries corporations are not persons. Before it was all settled in 2009, the towns passed ordinances that included the right of ecosystems to flourish and the right of citizens to self-governance, including the right to place groundwater in a public trust.[173]

Nestle backed down and was forced to withdraw its testing wells.

Since 2005, in Pennsylvania about a half dozen local governments have taken this route, abolishing the accumulated personhood "rights" and legal privileges claimed by corporations.[174]

But let's step back.

At our founding, "we the people" meant we real people, of course. Corporations are not mentioned in the Constitution; they came on the scene to further "we the people's" welfare. As agents to serve humanity, corporations themselves have no *inherent* rights; only people do.

Corporations do have numerous legal protections that we the people grant them and can revoke—including, for example, a corporation's limited legal liability, bankruptcy protection; virtual immortality (since their charters are rarely revoked), and a whole legal structure to protect their contracts.

These legal privileges (not to mention frequent huge public subsidies), added to their claim of inherent constitutional rights and their vastly superior resources relative to real people, mean corporations inevitably tilt to their benefit any political playing field of real people.

But democracy requires a level playing field. And that's what citizens of Humboldt County, California, for example, are going for.

There, Wal-Mart and the logging giant Maxxam had for years each spent hundreds of thousands of dollars to influence votes to serve their interests. So in mid-2006, a citizens' initiative banned from elections the use of money from non-locally owned corporations and other entities.[175] When outside corporate pressure led to a court challenge of the measure, many candidates for local office pledged to abide by it anyway, no matter what the court ultimately ruled.[176]

Note that if the efforts of Humboldt's citizens changed, at least locally, what's deemed acceptable in a democracy, that's a victory in itself.

### 5 At the same time, even some mega-corporations are redefining the bottom line to align profit with the prospering of the planet.

Increasing numbers of corporations are realizing that, actually, they're not required by their legal charters to seek only narrow, immediate gains for shareholders and CEOs, while leaving waste and destruction for the rest of us to clean up. Some are acknowledging mounting evidence that responsible businesses bring higher returns on average than do their less ethical competitors.[177] The two hundred companies of the World Business Council for Sustainable Development, one report showed, outperformed their respective stock exchanges by 15 to 25 percent during the early 2000s.[178]

Investor and buyer pressure is at play here, but so are some real human beings at the helm.

Consider the difference those human beings can make: GE, whose former head Jack Welch once scoffed at climate-change science and called mandated toxics clean-up unconstitutional, is now led by Jeffrey Immelt, who sees sustainable energy as a "business imperative." Since GE entered the wind energy business in 2002, it has increased its wind energy revenues by tenfold and has invested more than $850 million in wind turbine technology.[179] GE has also caught on that businesses need a level playing field to act on this good-business/good-planet sense, and that means government rules that apply to everyone. So GE is one of numerous companies advocating federally set carbon emissions restrictions.[180]

Americans' growing appetite for healthy food and sound corporate values has enabled Whole Foods Market to mushroom from founder John Mackey's 1980 Austin storefront to 195 stores, swallowing smaller competitors. Its "whole foods, whole people, whole planet" mission plays out in the company's emphasis on organic foods, support for local farmers, and use of renewable energy, along with its "Animal Compassionate Standards." And, while most CEO pay climbs skyward, Mackey as of 2007 receives one dollar annually.

Company values include giving workers a voice: "I could have clerked anywhere," a checkout person in Austin told me not long ago, "but here, we have a real voice. It's the team that decides who gets hired."

Yet Mackey resists unions that would allow workers an *independent* voice, and in 2003 described unions as "highly unethical."[181] And, in 2007, the Federal Trade Commission sued to stop what it saw as Mackey's anti-competitive attempt to buy his last big rival, Wild Oats. In 2009, Whole Foods settled the dispute by agreeing to sell thirty-two stores along with the Wild Oats brand.[182]

So, here's the question for Living Democracy: Can we learn to hold two seemingly contrary truths at once?

Can we cheer desperately needed, positive steps some corporations are taking and at the same time, without blinking, work to change the rules? Change them to disperse the over-the-top power of economic giants—for we know that their tight hold means they can deny workers real power, squeeze out independent businesses, and buy political clout, all contradicting democratic life?

### 6 Citizens are generating "local living economies" by standing up for their hometown businesses as they disperse economic power, reduce energy waste, and build community bonds.

"Buy Local or Bye-Bye Local." "Be a Local Lover."

You might spot these two bumper stickers in Bellingham, Washington these days, a city of sixty-seven thousand. And on storefronts, T-shirts, flyers, and newspaper pages in this bayside city, you could also see "Think Local, Buy Local, Be Local."

All are signs of Sustainable Connections, a coalition of locally owned businesses that in 2003 launched a "local first" campaign. By 2009 it had already succeeded in shifting three out of five residents to "thinking local first." Besides encouraging local provisioning, the efforts have sped green building, as well as helped spread renewable sources and the efficient use of energy in Bellingham.

Their success makes me think Sustainable Connections hit a nerve.

The budding "relocalize" movement is benefitting from and enhancing appreciation of the environmental benefits that come from shortening supply chains, as well as decentralizing economic life: A dollar spent in a locally owned business can generate three times more local economic activity than a dollar paid to a corporate chain.[183] Not to mention the trust and enjoyment that just happens when we buy from folks we know.

Eighty other cities have joined Bellingham in the fast-growing Business Alliance for Local Living Economies, including some big ones like Philadelphia, Santa Fe, and Grand Rapids, Michigan.[184]

In Bellingham, more than six hundred participating independent businesses now display a poster and a "buy local" decal in their windows. They give special thank-you cards to loyal customers and offer coupon books with discounts at member stores. And, to stir awareness of all great things local, in 2009 Sustainable Connections organized a county farm tour. Two thousand residents joined in the tour, offering "a wagon ride through the fields at Boxx Berry Farm with a berry shortcake in hand."

Who could resist?

Results from Bellingham's positive approach are rolling in. Sales with no middleman between producer and eater virtually doubled between 2002 and 2007, five times the state's average increase.

South of Bellingham in northern California is Mendocino County, where citizens also know a thing or two about standing up for their hometowns.

When an out-of-state developer managed to get an initiative before voters in the fall of 2009, locals got worried: Its passage would open the way for a megamall anchored by an 800,000-square-foot big-box store (think Wal-Mart or Costco), and citizens figured any opposition would be outspent, big-time.

But citizens of Ukiah, the chosen site, and in the wider county, weren't cowed. The grassroots group Save Our Local Economy, energized by four hundred volunteers, worked like crazy to defeat the initiative, Measure A.

Appealing directly to voters via the initiative meant that if the developer were successful, the project would be exempt from the California Environmental Quality Act, which covers everything from traffic to greenhouse gas emissions to impact on local businesses. Plus, the initiative meant the developer could avoid having to get the County Board of Supervisors' approval, which looked tough. The company knew that at least two supervisors were unlikely to go along.

*Wouldn't just snowing the citizens be a surer bet?*

The company used twenty mailings, plus a television and radio blitz, claiming that the project would create 700 new jobs and $1.7 million in new tax revenue.

But despite the down economy, most voters didn't buy it. The opposition garnered almost two thirds of the vote. This, despite the Ohio developer's spending a record-breaking $1.2 million—or about $133 dollars for every vote it got, outspending the citizens' group almost twelve dollars to one.

"We were sure that self-determination about how we grow our economy would prevail," Sheilah Rogers, a longtimer in Ukiah, told me. Possibly proving her right, those leading the opposition invited their neighbors into conversation; and in early 2010 they are busy researching industrial uses for the site that might include green-energy technology and green building-products companies.

Mendocino County citizens trusted their own and their neighbors' commonsense and backbone, stood up for democracy —and won.[185]

These stories could seem dreamy and irrelevant when corporate globalization can feel like a done deal. So please note: Locally owned, small businesses provide half the jobs and output in the U.S. private economy, says *Small-Mart Revolution* author Michael Shuman. He also notes that sole proprietorships—the legal form of most first-stage small businesses—are nearly three times more profitable than C-corporations, i.e., most global businesses.[186]

### 7 Businesses driven by their workers, members, or users of the companies' services are spreading worldwide—proving that markets can work splendidly without control by outside capital.

If you've ever shopped at Ace Hardware, you've used a cooperative business, owned by its thousands of member stores. If you've ever enjoyed Organic Valley yogurt, you've tasted the fruits of a farmer co-op.

In worker co-ops the owners are also the workers. And the impact can be huge.

Cooperative Home Care Associates in the Bronx has, in just twenty-five years, set a new standard for the home health aide industry—on which at least seven million American households depend. The co-op set out to transform the lives of aides who suffered overall lousy working conditions, with no benefits or regular hours. Born from a commitment to train poor women, many of whom had been receiving welfare, Cooperative Home Care Associates has grown to anchor a national cooperative network generating sixteen hundred home aide jobs, with decent pay and benefits and $60 million in annual revenue.

Florinda DeLeon, who went from entry-level worker to board member, told me that "being worker-owned means that we decide what's best for us." And "I don't ever have to think about being back on a welfare line."

In all their varieties—from worker- to consumer-owned, finance to farming—co-op membership worldwide has more than doubled in the last thirty years, now providing one hundred million jobs worldwide. That's one-fifth *more* than multinational corporations offer, says the Geneva-based International Co-operative Alliance.

Around the world, roughly 800 million people are now co-op members—outnumbering the number who own shares in publicly traded companies.[187] In 2009, three of the top six countries named by the World Economic Forum as having the most competitive economies were recently among the top four in share of sales contributed by co-ops: Finland, Switzerland, and Sweden. The overlap should erase any notion of an inevitable trade-off between democratic economic forms and economic efficiency.[188]

Are you surprised? I certainly was. But then again, when was the last time you saw a "co-op" section in your newspaper's "business pages"?[189]

- Perhaps most surprising for me is this comparison from India: There, more than 100,000 village dairy cooperatives, created and owned by nearly 13.5 million villagers—mainly women—provide about a fifth of the country's milk.[190] These worker-created jobs—ignored by global media—are roughly six times greater in number than the jobs generated by India's high-tech sector—regularly trumpeted by global media.[191]
- In Italy's Emilia Romagna region, a network of five thousand diverse cooperatives generates over 30 percent of the economic output, helping the region shine as one of Europe's wealthiest.
- In Argentina almost a quarter of the population takes part in a co-op. After the country's 2001 economic collapse shuttered thousands of businesses, many workers chose to keep the companies alive themselves. Workers "recovered" two hundred fifty firms that now employ thirteen thousand workers—some making twice their former wages. They're seeking to join Argentina's ten thousand other officially recognized cooperative factories.[192]
- In Colombia, the Saludcoop health care co-op, the nation's second largest employer, provides services to a quarter of the population.
- In Kuwait, 80 percent of all retail sales are rung up by the Union of Consumer Co-operative Societies.

Closer to home is Organic Valley, the brainchild of Wisconsin dairy farmers, distressed in the late 1980s to see their neighbors' farms folding while profits were going everywhere but to farmers. A handful of them decided an organic dairy cooperative could turn things around.

I admit, in 1988, sitting on a hard pew in a Viroqua, Wisconsin church listening to their vision—I was a doubter. I would never have guessed that in just over two decades their determination would birth a multimillion dollar company owned by almost fourteen hundred family farms in thirty-three states.[193] Organic Valley still lives by its democratic values, with profits returning to farmers and rural communities.

### 8 In thousands of schools and universities, students are learning democracy by doing it.

Students are moving from "community service," in which adults are in charge, to "apprentice citizenship," in which young people take ownership in hands-on learning. Most important, they experience their own power to make real, lasting improvements in their communities. From environmental restoration to improving their school food service, students in forty school districts in New England are learning by becoming community problem solvers as part of a movement led by Maine's KIDS Consortium.

"I realized I was saving lives. Now that's the shocking part," a Maine sixth grader told me after assuming leadership in a public safety campaign through KIDS. After being part of KIDS, the share of students expressing a sense of civic agency, measured by an independent review, jumped from about a third to half.[194]

Young people experiencing power as problem-solvers enhances academic achievement. In southern Ohio, as public school students in Federal Hocking High gained power—including equal voice with teachers in hiring faculty—the percentage going on to college climbed in a decade from 20 to 70 percent.

Old-fashioned student leadership for democracy on a broader scale is on the rise, too.

In local food movements, students from Santa Cruz to Cornell are leading the charge, linking local, sustainable, democratic food and farming to their school's food services. As part of the Real Food Challenge, students ask their schools to pledge that 20 percent of campus food will be "real"—sustainable, fairly produced, and local—by 2020. The young founders had hoped two hundred schools would be on board by the end of the first year, 2009. Instead, well over three hundred had joined in.

And students are gaining ground in holding school administrators accountable for buying products only from companies that play fair with their workers. Since 2000, the anti-sweatshop movement has spread to one hundred eighty-six colleges and universities.[195]

And its strategy has moved off campus, too.

In a remarkable 2009 win, students got sportswear giant Russell Athletic to commit to rehiring 1,200 workers in Honduras who had lost jobs because the company closed its factory after workers formed a union. Beyond convincing one hundred schools to boycott Russell, students picketed the N.B.A. finals because the league had a licensing agreement with Russell, and even "knocked on Warren Buffett's door in Omaha" because his company owns Russell's parent company.[196]

It took most of a year, but empowered students made it happen.

### 9 In law enforcement, community-based policing and restorative-justice approaches are reducing crime and healing communities.

In forty-seven states, volunteer citizen boards help decide the appropriate treatment for nonviolent transgressors, repairing the harm done and guiding violators' reintegration into the community, with huge public savings.[197]

Vermont was one of the first states to use the approach to save lives and money. In 2008, I got to sit in on a restorative justice session in Burlington with a young, hard-up couple who'd accepted some quick cash to fill a bogus prescription for an addict—and got caught. The board explained to the worried couple the community service they had to complete, but it had much more to offer: Being Burlington old-timers, the board members could share helpful insights about finding decent jobs. Who knows what difference this basic human connection has made for this couple's future.

Community policing—police and citizens partnering to reduce crime—was introduced in the 1980s but really took off during the Clinton administration. It is as much about keeping problems from entering the criminal justice doorway as it is about nabbing criminals. In Cincinnati, Ohio, almost one thousand city-trained volunteers, called Citizens on Patrol, cover twenty-four neighborhoods in the city.[198]

Thus, from political life to economic life to education to criminal justice, expectations of ourselves and others are changing, and the five qualities of Living Democracy noted in the previous chapter are showing up. For hundreds more stories in this vein—not random acts of sanity but innovations deepening and enlivening the very meaning of democracy—please see reading recommendations at the end of the book.

## WHY NOW? FOUR REVOLUTIONS

Despite the global economic and ecological downturn, making it harder for most of us to see possibility, at least four revolutions are underway, sea changes giving rise to Living Democracy beneath the turbulent waves.

### 1 A communications-knowledge revolution

Instantaneous global communication is allowing us to experience ourselves sharing one planet. This revolution is also exploding our access to knowledge—and with it our power—in part because it helps dissolve the scarcity paradigm.

Want access to world-class learning? No lack there.

Eighty-five percent of Massachusetts Institute of Technology course materials, for more than 2,000 courses, is now available free to anyone in the world through its "OpenCourseWare" at ocw.mit.edu. The site gets 1.5 million visits a month from all over the world. As professors' audiences explode, the quality of MIT teaching is improving, observed the system's former director Anne Margulies. More than two hundred universities worldwide are following MIT's lead and freely opening themselves to the world. Visit the Open Courseware Consortium, ocwconsortium.org.

Even Harvard is opening up, despite its former president Larry Summers reportedly dismissing open courseware as "one of the dumbest ideas I have ever heard." Presumably it did not fit his frame of protecting scarce intellectual property.

An icon in this demystification of knowledge—and its cooperative creation by volunteer users just wanting to contribute—is of course Wikipedia, with seven million articles. In English alone, it has twenty-five times the number of words as the *Encyclopedia Britannica*. When *Nature* magazine compared science articles in each for accuracy, it found on average four errors in Wikipedia and three in *Encyclopedia Britannica*.[199]

Now, my partner Richard Rowe and his colleagues are creating an online, open-access library of K-12 curricula for the world's children, allowing teachers and students anywhere to access and adapt the very best. It is called Open Learning Exchange, at ole.org.

Flouting the top-down control characteristic of Thin Democracy, this revolution thrives on people's need to contribute and cooperate.

Case in point?

The widening embrace of Linux—an open-source operating system—and the nascent rejection of Microsoft, with its top-down control of 90 percent of the world's software market. Not many years ago Munich, Germany, decided to convert thousands of government computers to Linux despite pleas by Microsoft's chief executive. Soon Brazil's government was on board, too, saving millions, and people across Latin America became leaders in the open-source movement. By the end of 2009 over 100 million downloads had occurred of Open Office, which amounts to a free version of Microsoft Office.

In the proprietary, top-down control world of software development, "The first step in using a computer was to promise not to help your neighbor. A cooperating community was forbidden," said Richard Stallman, founder of the open, non-proprietary software movement that created Linux. "The rule made by the owners of proprietary software was, 'If you share with your neighbor, you are a pirate.'"[200] So Stallman left that world and created the opposite: software rules and a culture that encourage mutual help and mutual learning. And it's catching on.

The communications revolution—with online independent news services proliferating and independent documentaries, such as "Food, Inc.," showing up in mainstream theaters—is also emboldening citizens.

Political candidates no longer control their message. Think blogs, cell phone videos, podcasts, and YouTube. Neither can governments. In mid-2009, for example, social media like Twitter enabled news of mass protests against Iran's disputed election of Mahmoud Ahmadinejad to spread worldwide; and in international solidarity, some message relayers altered their accounts' reported location to read "Tehran," hoping to confuse government monitors.

In other ways, new technologies are also making life tougher for officials keeping secrets, while for truth tellers, life is getting easier.

Consider Daniel Ellsberg.

Ellsberg became a hero for my generation when in 1971 he leaked what became known as the Pentagon Papers, classified material proving government deceit about the war in Vietnam. It took him six weeks to secretly photocopy seven thousand pages, and, once the *New York Times* had the material, three whole months passed before it was published.

Contrast Ellsberg's effort with that of Treasury Secretary Paul O'Neill. Fired by President Bush in 2002, he walked out the door with a CD-ROM containing nineteen thousand documents. Some of the most revealing material almost immediately appeared on the Web.[201]

Big difference.

Transparency is not just a new buzzword. It matters. It makes anonymity—one thing sure to lead to no good—impossible. And new communications tools suddenly transform "transparency" into *useable* information.

Visit scorecard.org, key in your ZIP code, and find out not only which companies are polluting your town but what they are spewing into your water and air. When I did this, I was in for a shock: A company I jog by regularly ranks among my county's top twenty polluters. This Web-based service is possible only because the 1986 Right-to-Know law required corporate disclosure of certain types of toxic chemicals. That info went into an accessible online inventory.

In the first seven years after the inventory's 1988 launch, corporate releases of listed chemicals dropped by 45 percent, and in the first fifteen, hazardous chemicals stored on site fell almost 60 percent.[202] Here, required transparency alone—made useful because of the communications revolution—arguably produced history's fastest ever voluntary corporate environmental improvement.

## 2 A networking revolution

The Internet is also directly enabling citizen campaigns and enlivening global collaboration among citizen movements.

For starters, they become visible to one other. Environmentalist Paul Hawken's brainchild wiserearth.org profiles over one hundred ten thousand citizen organizations all over the world.

One moment in 1999 signaled possibilities to come: It was the birth of "Indymedia" during citizen protests against the World Trade Organization in Seattle. In that first week, online Independent Media Center's two million viewers eclipsed visits to CNN. Using open-source software allowing anyone to publish, the center's sites—all known as "Indymedia"— have spread to more than a dozen countries; its hub, now in eight languages, gets as many as one hundred thousand hits a day.[203]

Ten years later, the Internet made possible the biggest—geographically speaking—coordinated political action in history: October 24, 2009. Starting with a handful of Middlebury college students, and author-activist Bill McKibben in the lead, 350.org ignited actions to address the climate crisis in 5,281 spots around the world—from the pyramids in Egypt to the steps of the Sydney Opera House to the beaches of Yemen.

The power of citizen networking is just beginning to be felt. It helped achieve the 1997 Mine-Ban Treaty, and abetted the historically rapid ratification of the 2003 Global Tobacco Treaty, the world's first public health treaty I mentioned earlier.

## 3 A revolution in human dignity

It's easy to miss how revolutionary is the view that each human life is of inherent worth and thus entitled to a voice in our common destiny. Even in many of today's "old democracies," women won the right to vote so recently that some alive today were born without it. And just since 1980, citizens in forty-seven more countries have gained democratic rights, says a U.N. report.[204]

The right to food—essential to human dignity—is now enshrined in the constitutions of twenty-two nations.

Other signs of this revolution?

In the opening chapter, I argued that continuing to evolve punishment for transgressions against humanity is key to our species' growing up. In that light, establishing the International Criminal Court in 2002 was a huge step. With one hundred and ten member countries, despite strong resistance from the United States, it's now pursuing four crimes-against-humanity cases, including the Darfur genocide.

And, in Europe, if you believe your basic human rights to have been violated without proper redress within your home country, you now have a place to turn. It is the supra-national European Court of Human Rights, a Strasbourg-based tribunal to which any state body of the forty-six country signatories can also bring a claim. In its current form, just since 1998, the court has issued judgments that range from holding the Russian military responsible for torturing Chechens, to compensation for a Polish woman barred from ending her pregnancy even though giving birth, doctors told her, could leave her disabled (and did).

I'll understand if you think it's a stretch to claim a "revolution in human dignity" in a world experiencing genocide; or in a world where twelve to twenty-seven million people, nearly half of them children, are enslaved—forced to work by threat of violence for little or nothing; or in a world where human trafficking is a booming $32 billion business.

Yet slavery fighter Kevin Bales sees change: "[W]e don't have to win the moral argument; no one is trying to justify it anymore."[205] That's a revolution.

## 4 An ecological revolution

The fourth wind in the sails of Living Democracy also involves our consciousness—ecological imagery seeping deep into us over the last four decades to profound effect. We're coming to see that ecology is not about "Nature" apart from us. We and the butterflies are in this together. And such lovely metaphors suddenly become very real—and not so lovely—when we learn that, for example, on some days almost one-quarter of pollutants in Los Angeles's air come from coal plants and cars in China and dust from deforestation in Asia.[206]

Ecological consciousness also tells us there is no "away" to which we can toss used goods. And there is no escape, either: The damage we create as we heat the planet or deny basic food and health care to billions is damage to our ecological and social tissue that none can avoid. Now, there's motivation.

Through ecology's lens, we can perceive our power in new ways, too, as I discuss in the coming chapter. Since interdependence isn't a nice wish, *it is what is*, there can be no single action, isolated and contained. All actions create ripples—not just downward through hierarchical flows but outward globally through webs of connectedness. And we never know what those ripples might be. Beneath our awareness, perhaps, we are coming to realize that our acts do matter, all of them, everywhere, all the time.

"Yeah, yeah, each action counts, but we still must choose," I can hear a reader sighing. Do I engage right in my own backyard like the Kansans who began this chapter? Or do I go national—helping, say, to purge money's corrupting grip from politics with the YouStreet folks? What about climate chaos—it's global?

Local versus national versus global—this frame gets us nowhere. Rules of our economy and of politics set nationally and globally, now divide and disempower people locally. Yet many of us will become convinced that these rules can be made fair only as we experience change right in our own communities. So there is no chicken or egg—all have to be happening at once. And are. The real question is not about the level of our engagement but whether our choices fire our passions and reverse the *Spiral of Powerlessness* for ourselves and others—an exploration at the heart of Chapter 10.

But given the incessant stoking of fear in our society and the top-down control built into Thin Democracy, where is our power for this radical assertion of basic common sense?

To discover it, we may have to rethink the meaning of power, too.

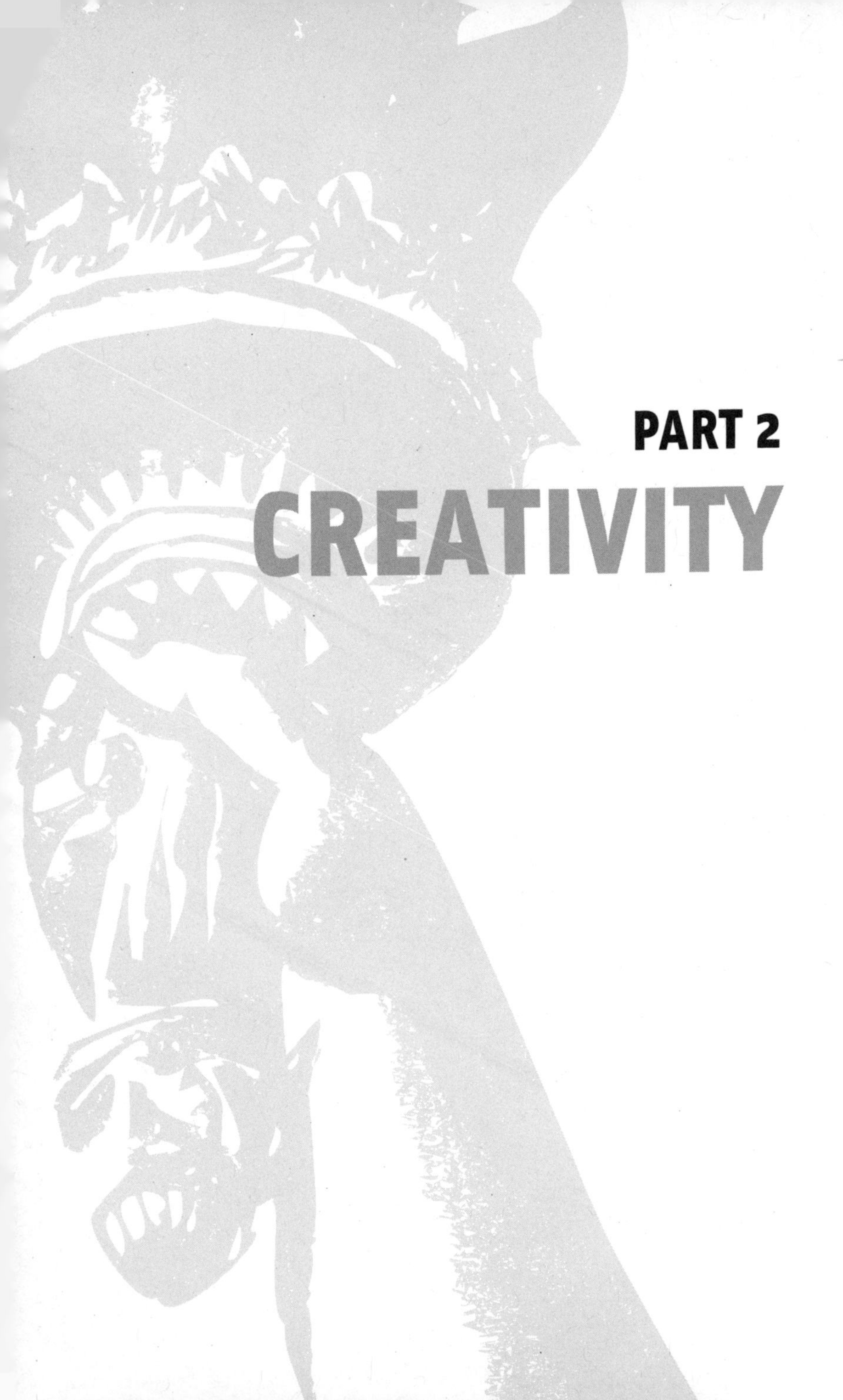

# PART 2
# CREATIVITY

# 5 POWER INVISIBLE

*People think "power...oh, that's bad."*
*But powerlessness, that's really bad!*

—MARGARET MOORE, CITIZEN ORGANIZER, FORT WORTH, TEXAS, 1992

A Massachusetts teacher I once knew asked his tenth graders to blurt out the first words that came to mind on hearing the word "power." They said, "money," "parents," "guns," "bullies," "Adolf Hitler," and "Mike Tyson." And in my workshops with adults, I've heard similar words, plus "fist," "law," "corrupt," and "politicians." Often "men" pops out, too.

As long as we conceive of power as the capacity to exert one's will over another, it is something to be wary of. Power can manipulate, coerce, and destroy. And as long as we are convinced we have none, power will always look negative. Even esteemed journalist Bill Moyers recently reinforced a view of power as categorically negative. "The further you get from power," he said, "the closer you get to the truth."[207]

But power means simply our capacity to act. "Power is necessary to produce the changes I want in my community," Margaret Moore of Allied Communities of Tarrant (ACT) in Fort Worth, Texas—my hometown—told me. I've found many Americans returning power to its original meaning—"to be able." From this lens, we each have power—often much more power than we think.

## ONE CHOICE WE DON'T HAVE

In fact, we have no choice about whether to be world changers. If we accept ecology's insights that we exist in densely woven networks, as just noted, then we must also accept that every choice we make sends out ripples, even if we're not consciously choosing. *So the choice we have is not whether, but only how, we change the world.* All this means that public life is not simply what officials and other "big shots" have, as I've tried to capture in *Idea 2* in Chapter 3.

Related evidence of our power is so obvious it is often overlooked.

Human beings show up in *radically* different notches on the "ethical scale" depending on the culture in which we live. In Japan, "only" 15 percent of men beat their spouses. In many other countries, over half do. The murder rate in the United States is four times higher than in Western Europe, Canada, Australia, and Japan.

Plus, behavior can change quickly. Germany moved from a country in which millions of its citizens went along with mass murder to become in a single generation one of the world's more respected nations. Here's an incomparably less consequential but still telling example: In only a decade, 1992 to 2002, U.S. high school students who admitted to cheating on a test at least once in a year climbed by 21 percent to three quarters of all surveyed.[208]

So what do these differences and the speed of change in behavior tell us? That it is *culture*, not fixed aspects of human nature, which largely determines the prevalence of cooperation or brutality, honesty or deceit. And since we create culture through our daily choices, then we do, each of us, wield enormous power.

Let me explore related, empowering findings of science that also confirm our power.

## MIRRORS IN OUR BRAINS

Recent neuroscience reveals our interdependence to be vastly greater than we'd ever imagined.

In the early 1990s, neuroscientists were studying the brain activity of monkeys, particularly in the part of the brain's frontal lobe associated with distinct actions, such as reaching or eating. They saw specific neurons firing for specific activities. But then they noticed something they didn't expect at all: The very same neurons fired when a monkey was simply *watching* another monkey perform the action.

"Monkey see, monkey do" suddenly took on a whole new meaning for me. Since we humans are wired like our close relatives, when we observe someone else, our own brains are simultaneously experiencing at least something of what that person is experiencing. More recent work studying humans has borne out this truth.[209]

These copycats are called "mirror neurons," and their significance is huge. We do walk in one another's shoes, whether we want to or not.

> *[Our] intimate brain-to-brain link-up… lets us affect the brain—and so the body—of everyone we interact with, just as they do us.*
>
> —DANIEL GOLEMAN,
> *SOCIAL INTELLIGENCE: THE NEW SCIENCE OF HUMAN RELATIONSHIPS*[210]

We literally experience and therefore co-create one another, moment to moment. For me, our "imprintability" is itself a source of hope. We can be certain that our actions, and perhaps our mental states, register in others. We change anyone observing us. That's power.

And we never know who's watching. Just think: It may be when we feel most marginalized and unheard, but still act with resolve, that someone is listening or watching and their life is forever changed.

As I form this thought, the face of Wangari Maathai comes to mind. A Kenyan, Wangari planted seven trees on Earth Day in Nairobi in 1977 to honor seven women environmental leaders there. Then, over two decades, she was jailed, humiliated, and beaten for her environmental activism, but her simple act ultimately sparked a movement in which those seven trees became forty-five *million*, all planted by village women across Kenya.

In the fall of 2004, when Maathai got the call telling her she had just won the Nobel Peace Prize, her first words were: "I didn't know anyone was listening." But, evidently, a lot of people were beginning to listen, from tens of thousands of self-taught tree planters in Kenya to the Nobel committee sitting in Oslo.

From there I flash back to a conversation with João Pedro Stédile, a founder of the largest and perhaps most effective social movement in this hemisphere—Brazil's Landless Workers' Movement, enabling some of world's poorest people to gain nearly twenty million acres of unused land. During the military regime in the early 1980s in Brazil, even gathering a handful of people was risky.

Who helped motivate João Pedro? It was Cesar Chavez and the U.S. farm workers' struggle, he told me.

I'll bet Chavez never knew, or even imagined, his example was powerful enough to jump continents.

Just as important, the findings of neuroscience also give us insight as to how to change and empower ourselves. They suggest that a great way is to place ourselves in the company of those we want most to be like. For sure, we'll become more like them.

Thus, whom we choose to spend time with as friends, colleagues, and partners may be our most important choices. And "spending time" means more than face-to-face contact. What we witness on TV, in films, and on the Internet, what we read and therefore imagine—all are firing mirror neurons in our brains and forming us.

As the author of *Diet for a Small Planet*, I'm associated with a focus on the power of what we put into our mouths. But what we let into our minds equally determines who we become. So why not choose an empowering new diet? I've included my own menu suggestions in "Recommended Reading" at the book's end.

## POWER ISN'T A FOUR LETTER WORD

Power is an idea. And in our culture it's a stifling idea. We're taught to see power as something fixed—we either have it or we don't. But if power is our capacity to get things done, then even a moment's reflection tells us we can't create much alone. From there, power becomes something we human beings develop together—*relational power*. And it's a lot more fun.

| IDEA 3: Rethinking Power | |
|---|---|
| POWER **IS** | POWER **CAN BE** |
| Zero-sum. It strengthens some people at the expense of others. It divides what already exists. | Mutually expanding. It builds the capacities of all involved. It is creative, generating new strengths and new possibilities. |
| A one-way force: either you have it, or you don't. Life boils down to the powerful versus the powerless. | A give-and-take, two-way relationship. No one is ever completely powerless because each person's actions affect others. |
| Limiting, intimidating, and scary. | Freeing. |
| Controlling. | Collaborative. |
| Rigid, static. | Dynamic, always changing. |
| Derived mostly from laws, status, force, and wealth. | Derived from relationships, knowledge, experience, numbers, organization, creativity, vision, perseverance, discipline, humor, and more. |
| About what I can do or get *right now*. | Mindful of creating and sustaining relational power over time. |

"Relational" suggests that power can expand for many people simultaneously. It's no longer a harsh, zero-sum concept—the more for you, the less for me. Growth in one person's power can enhance the power of others. *Idea 3* contrasts our limited, negative view of power with a freeing, relational view.

Let me tell you one story of relational power.

In the 1970s, pollution in Chattanooga, Tennessee, was so bad that drivers had to turn on their headlights at noon to cut through it. But in the 1990s, this once-and-again-charming city—famous for its choo-choos—went from racially divided ugly duckling to swan, winning international awards and the envy of its neighbors.

The city's rebirth sprang in part from big investments in the city's cultural renewal, including the world's largest freshwater aquarium, attracting over a million visitors a year. It also included a renovated theater involving one thousand volunteers annually and a new riverfront park.

But all these great breakthroughs weren't the city fathers' ideas.

Twenty years ago, fifty spunky, frustrated citizens declared that the old ways of making decisions weren't working and drew their fellow residents—across race and class lines—into a twenty-week series of brainstorming sessions they called "visioning."

Their goal was hardly modest—to save their city by the end of the century. They called it Vision 2000. They drew up thirty-four goals, formed action groups, sought funding, and rolled up their sleeves.

By 1992, halfway along, the visioners had already achieved a remarkable 85 percent of their goals. Smog had been defeated, tourism was booming thanks to the new aquarium, crime was down, and jobs and low-income housing were on the rise. People stayed downtown after dark, and the refurbished riverside had become an oak-dappled Mecca.

Chattanoogans didn't stop there. In 1992, a citywide meeting to shape a school reform agenda drew not the small crowd expected but fifteen hundred people, who generated two thousand suggestions.

By now the approach has seeped its way into the city's culture. In 2002, to plan a big waterfront project, three hundred people participated in a "charrette" where teams used rolls of butcher paper to draw what they wanted to see happen.

"Basically, everything we do, any major initiative in Chattanooga, now involves public participation," said Karen Hundt, who works for a joint city-county planning agency. From Atlanta to West Springfield, Massachusetts, from Bahrain to Zimbabwe, citizens taken by Chattanooga's story are rewriting it to suit their own needs.

Here power is not a pie to be sliced up. It grows as citizens join together, weaving relationships essential to sustained change.

## RELATIONAL POWER'S UNDER APPRECIATED SOURCES

We commonly think of power in the form of official status or great wealth or force—only available to a few of us—but take a moment to mull over these twelve sources of relational power available to any one of us.[211]

- **Building relationships of trust.** Thirty-five hundred congregations—Catholics, Protestants, Jews, and some Evangelicals and Muslims—are dues-paying members of one hundred thirty-three religious networks nationwide. These local federations with members adding up to as many as three million Americans are successfully tackling problems that range from poverty wages to failing schools. Their genius is what they call "one-on-one" organizing strategies. These involve face-to-face meetings allowing ordinary people to discover their own capacities because someone—finally—is listening.[212]
- **Ability to analyze power and self-interest.** One such organization, Communities Organized for Public Service in San Antonio, analyzes corporate interests before bringing corporations into dialogue on job-training reform.
- **Knowledge.** National People's Action documents banks' racial "redlining" in lending and helps to pass the federal Community Reinvestment Act, which has brought over a trillion dollars into poor neighborhoods. Workers at South Mountain Company in Massachusetts buy the company and apply knowledge from their direct experience to make it profitable and incorporate energy-efficient methods.
- **Numbers of people.** The congregation-based Industrial Areas Foundation is able to gather together thousands for public "actions," commanding the attention of lawmakers.
- **Discipline.** Young people in the Youth Action Program—precursor to the nationwide YouthBuild—handle themselves with

such decorum at a New York City Council meeting that officials are moved to respond to the group's request for support.

- **Vision.** In the Merrimack Valley Project in Massachusetts, some businesses "catch" the citizens' vision of industry responsive to community values and change their positions.
- **Diversity.** Memphis's Shelby County Interfaith Organization identifies distinct black and white interests on school reform and multiplies its impact by addressing both sets in improving Memphis schools.
- **Creativity.** Citizens in St. Paul devise their own neighborhood network to help the elderly stay out of nursing homes. Regular folks in San Antonio devise a new job training program that's become a national model.
- **Persistence.** Members of ACORN, a four-hundred-thousand-member-strong, low-income people's organization, stand in line all night in the mid '90s in order to squeeze out paid banking lobbyists for seats in the congressional hearing room during debates over the Community Reinvestment Act. That 1977 law has helped stabilize many poor neighborhoods. (In 2009, when mistakes within ACORN led not just to efforts to hold the guilty accountable but to a hostile attempt to destroy the organization, my thoughts turned to the thousands of low-income people who have found their voices through ACORN's training and courageous actions.)
- **Humor.** Kentuckians for the Commonwealth stage a skit at the state capitol. In bed are KFTC members portraying legislators and their farmer chairperson pretending to be a coal lobbyist.

They pass big wads of fake cash under the covers. Grabbing media attention, they get their reform measure passed.

- **Chutzpah—nerve.** Sixth graders in Amesville, Ohio, don't trust the EPA to clean up after a toxic spill in the local creek, so they form themselves into the town's water quality control team and help get the job done.
- **Mastering the arts of democracy.** Organizations of the Industrial Area Foundation network, over fifty nationwide, evaluate and reflect—often right on the spot—following each public action or meeting. They ask: How do you feel? How did each spokesperson do? Did we meet our goals? A seasoned organizer will also try to use the opportunity to deepen understanding of what the organization sees as the "universals" of public life, such as relational power.

## DROPS COUNT

Sadly, though, many of us remain blind to such a promising reframing of possibility. Imagining ourselves powerless, we disparage our acts as mere drops in the bucket or as, well, useless. But think about it: Buckets fill up really fast on a rainy night. Feelings of powerlessness come *not* from seeing oneself as a drop; they arise when we can't perceive the bucket at all. Thus, to uproot feelings of powerlessness, we can work to define and shape the bucket—*to consciously construct a frame that gives meaning to our actions.*

As you now know, for me a "bucket" that both contains and gives meaning to our creative, positive acts is Living Democracy. It springs from and meets humanity's common and deep emotional and spiritual needs. So, I wonder: In a world torn apart by sectarian division, could Living Democracy become a uniting *civic* vision complementing our religious and spiritual convictions—a nonsectarian yet soul-satisfying pathway out of the current morass?

I can't be certain, of course, but I think so.

And then again, I ask myself often: *Whatever* the odds of reversing our global catastrophe, is there a more invigorating way to live than that of making democracy a way of life?

In answering that question negatively, I *am* certain.

# 6 THE ART OF POWER

*I wonder whether Americans still believe liberty has to be learned and that its skills are worth learning. Or have they been deluded by two centuries of rhetoric into thinking that freedom is "natural" and can be taken for granted?*

—BENJAMIN BARBER, AUTHOR, *STRONG DEMOCRACY*
DIRECTOR, CIVWORLD[213]

With the collapse of the Soviet Union in 1989, those outside marveled at the staggering pace of change there. Communism's political institutions—seemingly as rigid and immovable as the mammoth steel and cement structures that housed them—simply collapsed. Command economies gave way to the market. And the world celebrated as democracy seemed to be breaking out all over.

Yet as the 1990s wore on and the euphoria wore off, it became clear that behind these highly visible structural changes, the reality of people's daily lives was in many ways worsening quickly. Even life expectancy began to fall. The KGB, the feared Soviet secret police, didn't dissolve exactly; it morphed into the Russian FSB that many have experienced as a state-sanctioned mafia. And soon, Vladimir Putin started acting way too much like a czar.

Similarly, consider the consequences of the U.S. invasion of Iraq, ostensibly to bring democracy. The United States played a big role in shaping the country's new constitution, but even after as many as 654,000 deaths directly and indirectly linked to the war, according to a Johns Hopkins study, violence continues.[214]

Formal institutions can change dramatically, but that is not enough. Something else is needed.

But what is that something else?

It's not nearly as clear-cut or visible as the structures of government or the rules on the books. But that something else may be just as important to democracy. (After all, the old Soviet Union had a superb bill of rights...on paper.)

I call what's needed the *culture of democracy*.

As noted in the previous chapter, it is not law but culture's power that explains so much of our social existence—why Western Europe, for instance, can register a GDP per person only two thirds of the size of the United States' and still enjoy quality of life measures exceeding ours.[215] Or why teen pregnancy rates here are *four times* those in France and Germany.[216]

To a large extent, culture is a set of expectations. How will we behave toward one another? What can we expect from our fellow citizens? What does the community expect of us? What are the unspoken rules that we just assume will be followed in our daily interactions? In one sense, *a culture of democracy can be defined as one that builds trust.*

Reading that last sentence, one's reaction might understandably be: Trust? Forget it. Sales of locks, guns, and gates are booming. True, as fear is stoked, trust shrinks, but upon even a moment's reflection, we realize that trust is still ubiquitous. Maybe, like cooperation, so ubiquitous we don't often register it. Every time we put a bite of food in our mouths, we put our lives into the hands of a supply chain of strangers. Every time the light turns green and we press the pedal, we trust strangers who are also capable of doing us great harm.

Societies couldn't function without trust. The challenge of our lives is re-creating and deepening trust by engaging directly with others to create a culture that works for all of us.

## DEMOCRACY'S ARTS

The people from all walks of life you meet in this book are shaping a democratic culture offering them much greater rewards. At the same time they're strengthening personal qualities that, in turn, make them even more effective. Skills that make possible this self-reinforcing pattern I call the "arts of democracy." *Idea 4* lists ten of these. At smallplanet.org you'll find a fuller "how-to" guide, *Doing Democracy*.[217]

I choose the term "art" quite deliberately, seeking to elevate the notion of democratic practice to something that is prized. "Art" doesn't have to that something at which only the talented few can succeed. Developing an art is possible for each of us, but it can't be learned by rote or practiced by formula. In any art, individuals add their own twists; and its practice calls on not one but many of our faculties.

Most important, an art can be *learned*. In fact, there is no end to the learning.

## IDEA 4: Ten Arts of Democracy

**1. ACTIVE LISTENING**
Encouraging the speaker and searching for meaning

**2. CREATIVE CONFLICT**
Confronting others in ways that produce growth for all

**3. MEDIATION**
Facilitating interaction to help people in conflict hear one

**4. NEGOTIATION**
Problem solving that meets some key interests of all involved

**5. POLITICAL IMAGINATION**
Re-imaging our futures according to our values

**6. PUBLIC DIALOGUE**
Public talk on matters that concern us all

**7. PUBLIC JUDGMENT**
Public decision making that allows citizens to make choices they are willing to help implement

**8. CELEBRATION**
Expressing joy and gratitude for what we learn as well as what we achieve

**9. EVALUATION AND REFLECTION**
Assessing and incorporating the lessons we learn through action

**10. MENTORING**
Supportively guiding others in learning these arts of public life

## THE POWER OF SIMPLY LISTENING

The first art of old-style politics or old-style management is drawing up one's manifesto, plan, or agenda and then selling it to others. The first art of Living Democracy is simply listening.

But is it really so simple?

At its most complete, active listening suggests putting oneself in another's shoes, seeing the world—even if for just a fleeting moment—from the other's vantage point. We can then begin to perceive links to our own interests, making common action possible.

Earlier I recounted how COPS (Communities Organized for Public Service), a citizen organization in San Antonio, reacted to its frustration at high unemployment rates among Hispanics. COPS members were upset because their city's biggest employers were bringing in outsiders to fill jobs.

COPS might have simply staged an angry protest. Instead, it invited corporate leaders to the table. COPS members listened. They listened to the concerns of those they might have seen only as adversaries. They listened to the companies' CEOs tell them of their own frustrations in not being able to find qualified employees locally. COPS members discovered a common interest with the business leaders: improving the city's job training efforts. From there, COPS went on to develop an innovative redesign of the city's job training programs, which the city council passed unanimously.

Active listening also spurs creativity.

That's why English professor emeritus Peter Elbow at the University of Massachusetts came up with an active-listening teaching tool. He calls it "The Believing Game." Our culture overemphasizes the importance of critical thinking, Peter believes. We're taught to find flaws in *any* argument. But this approach can make even the best idea look bad. A creative idea with far-reaching advantages can be ignored just because it contradicts conventional wisdom or is poorly stated.

To avoid this risk, Peter argues, we can learn to make a conscious, disciplined effort to *pretend* a new idea is the best proposal, and then see what we notice.[218] What's required is a special kind of active listening—the temporary suspension of disbelief. Dropping our tendency to first identify problems frees our creativity.

Active listening changes the speaker, too.

In private life, when we go to a friend for advice and that friend simply listens, we're often amazed to discover it is we ourselves who have the answers. We may have had them all along, but formulating our ideas to make ourselves clear to someone else enables us suddenly to become aware of those answers for the first time.

The same possibility exists in public life. In North Carolina, for example, the Listening Project bases its community improvement work on hundreds of in-depth, one-on-one interviews with people in their homes. Instead of quick check-off surveys, organizers ask open-ended questions about people's values and concerns. In one home, a middle-aged white man complained that the biggest problem he saw was the noisy black teenagers who hung out on the streets and caused trouble.

On a simple survey, that one comment might have gotten him labeled a racist. But the organizers just listened. They didn't argue. As the man talked, he began to reflect, as well. By the end of the interview, he himself had restated—and re-understood—his neighborhood's problem as its lack of decent recreational and job opportunities for young people.

While we think of listening as passive, this story suggests much more. The very experience of being truly listened to can profoundly change the speaker.

## CONFLICT AS CREATIVE

Living democracy means ongoing change, and change implies, minimally, that somebody thinks it's possible to improve upon the status quo. No big shock, then, that somebody else feels criticized.

So change entails conflict. Yet, while Americans flock to action movies and stay glued to reality TV, in our real lives, most of us abhor conflict. I am convinced it's not just fear of a bruised ego; it's a primal fear of losing standing in our "tribe," of being cast out into the wilderness, as I pick up again in Chapter 9.

Our aversion to conflict pops out in the sentiments of parents who brag about their "good kids" who "never give me problems." Or school principals whose extra praise is reserved for teachers maintaining the most obedient classrooms. Or bosses who make clear that it's those that "don't make waves" who'll be rewarded.

Fear of bucking these messages stops us from acting on what we know we want. So creatively *using* conflict is a key to creating the societies we want. That's why I'm impressed by sophisticated citizen organizations that train and mentor in this art of democracy. They are teaching that conflict means engagement—that something real is in motion. It's an opening, not a closing. They appreciate what James Surowiecki writes in his bestseller *The*

*Wisdom of Crowds*: "[T]he simple fact of making a group diverse makes it better at problem solving."[219]

The huge congregation-based Industrial Areas Foundation network make rehearsing and re-rehearsing for any contentious public encounter part of its M.O.

In Massachusetts, the two thousand members of Lawrence Community Works, bringing life back to what once was a thriving industrial town, have created their own members' training program. It's called the Poder ("to be able" in Spanish) Institute. Classes run every Saturday afternoon, in sessions of six months.

Using what it calls "network organizing," this community development corporation focuses less on bricks-and-mortar rebuilding than on "organic connections" among people, and then invests in strengthening and multiplying those connections. Out of these relationships comes the rebuilding of community. "Embedded in our teaching is our understanding that conflict can be used for good and is necessary for growth," the group's organizing director Alma Couverthié told me.

## The art of surfacing conflict

One of the biggest differences between Living Democracy and Thin Democracy is whether conflict is buried or surfaced.

Because Living Democracy, and ultimately the survival of much of life, now depends on our *not* going along, not cooperating with assumptions that violate our deeper needs and wisdom, surfacing conflict is a core skill in effectively living democracy.

Living democracy means inclusion, and what is another word for inclusion? It is diversity, diversity of all types making contact. And what is the root meaning of conflict? Collision–so we could think of Living Democracy as the richness of colliding differences.

Therefore, just as important as creatively resolving conflict, truly living democracy means creatively surfacing conflict.

In Des Moines, Iowa, several years ago Sally Riggs got involved with Iowa Citizens for Community (Iowa CCI) after her family had been deceived by a predatory lender.

She was reluctant at first, but with coaching, Sally gained confidence and skills.

"Before the meetings [with the mortgage company] I used to feel like I was going to be sick, I was so nervous. But the rehearsals helped. We would go to the group's office and practice making our case in their old meeting room. Joe or Tyler, staff organizers, would play the part of the executive across the table. They'd throw at us all the arguments we thought they would use. We did that as often as we could, and then, an hour before the real meeting, we would do it one last time. There weren't too many meetings when something came up that we hadn't seen coming and got ourselves ready for."

All this worked for Sally when her big day came in Chicago. When one financial executive seemed to dismiss her argument, Sally was hardly tongue-tied. She recalls saying: "And how would you like it if your five-year-old girl couldn't answer the phone in her own home because she was scared to?"

While she had always been petrified of the mortgage company, that changed when a bus full of other victims and supporting members of Iowa CCI refused to leave the office of one of the worst lenders. The police, summoned by the executives, advised the cowering mortgage execs that perhaps they should solve the people's problems. They did.

Naturally, we fear power imbalances. If our adversary is someone we perceive as holding power by his or her very position, how do we balance it out? With both the power of knowledge we bring in the door and the power of our numbers—the strength we communicate and feel by having allies at our side.

## KIDS LEARN CONFLICT IS OKAY

Although conflict in schools that spirals into ugly violence grabs the headlines, thousands of schools are learning to deter violence and turn conflict into strength.

They train both students and teachers to mediate differences among their peers in a movement unheard of only twenty years ago. It works this way: students volunteer for mediation training—typically fifteen hours covering active listening, paraphrasing, reframing, and role playing. The new mediators promote their services and encourage their peers to bring unresolved disputes to them. Schools often find many more students volunteering than they can use.

"One teacher typically becomes the point person," Richard Cohen, a founder of the movement, explained to me. "When a conflict arises, this person chooses two students who might be right for those two parties. Some schools handle three hundred to four hundred cases a year, and a mature program reaches 10 percent of the student body each year." In only a decade, the number of participating schools has jumped from five thousand to between ten and fifteen thousand.

"In a new high school in Lincoln-Sudbury, Massachusetts, they even built into the plans a suite of rooms specifically for mediation," Richard said. "That's how far we've come.

"What I love about mediation training is that it puts students themselves in charge of an aspect of school that is so important to them—their relationships. And all types, not just the honor roll students, are involved."

> *We teach kids that conflict is normal, that there's no way to avoid it, and that it can be positive.*
>
> –RICHARD COHEN, FOUNDER, SCHOOL MEDIATION ASSOCIATES

"It's not unusual to find that the average student is a better mediator than the adult. Effectiveness depends on being good at reading people, making them comfortable. You can get a seventeen-year-old with a ton of that kind of interpersonal intelligence," Richard explained.

"We ask kids whether they've ever felt closer to someone *after* going through a conflict. And a lot of hands go up. They get it. We also teach that conflict can be resolved cooperatively, not always competitively."

As with many breakthroughs creating a culture of democracy as a lived practice, school mediation now has a long enough track record to measure its success. A 2003 report shows that in more than nine out of ten cases, school mediation achieves a resolution, and disputants express satisfaction at almost as high a rate.[220]

As we learn to practice the arts of democracy, it may dawn on us that engagement is not, as we've been told, the spinach we must eat to move on to the dessert of personal freedom. Rather, it feels like another way of talking about the unending personal growth that makes life worth living. Or, as one feisty citizen expressed it to me: "The fun of power."

# 7 TALKING DEMOCRACY

*We have a language of Marxism and we have a language of capitalism, but we have no language of democracy. And we cannot create what we cannot name.*

—LAWRENCE GOODWYN, HISTORIAN

Throughout I've stressed the power of "frame," the lens through which we interpret our world. But what creates our frame? Largely, the stories we hear.

Today in America, Thin Democracy advocates are powerfully shaping those stories. Its proponents have weakened rules protecting us from monopoly power, including media monopoly—just six corporations now control most U.S. media outlets.[221] They have also succeeded in eliminating the media "fairness doctrine," which, for most of four decades, ensured at least a modicum of opinion balance, and embodied the ethic that media is not merely a commodity but also a public good.

As a result, nine out of ten of radio talk shows now trumpet one central story: government is our enemy.[222] Those, including, for example, Franklin Roosevelt, who view basic economic security as essential to freedom and to be protected by government, are portrayed as virtual traitors; they deserve to be attacked, even shouted down, as un-American liars and socialists. Over the last three decades, spokespeople with a Thin Democracy worldview have spun their own language: "the leave-us-alone coalition," "tax-and-spend liberals," "death tax," "death panels," "government takeover of health care"—all phrases fueling hostility and fear.

Because honest dialogue, including "fair fighting," is at the heart of democracy, we face a national crisis. Demagoguery—the attempt to gain power by appealing to people's prejudices and fears—is a hallmark of fascism. It stymies common problem solving, now needed more than ever, not only because it manipulates us but because it repels people. Reacting to extreme political ads, my mom put this sardonic title on an opinion piece she wrote in the early 1980s: "I Get It: They Just Don't Want Us to Vote."

So how do we confront this national crisis?

Several thoughts.

We can call for a national, bipartisan commission to establish a code of conduct for political discourse and to monitor, judge, and publicize the cumulative records of violations by public figures, including those in the media. That standard might be simple: adherence to truthful speech about evidence, public actions, and opinions, not character. The Internet offers opportunity for public discussion of an evolving standard. We can ask an institution, such as the League of Women Voters, the Annenberg Foundation, or the National Civic League to take this on.

We can hold ourselves to a high standard and take responsibility for standing up to anti-democratic fear mongering and dishonest speech, wherever we encounter it.

Those appalled by the "town hall tirades" in the summer of 2009 seemed blindsided. Now, knowing the possibility of such intimidation tactics, those standing for fair debate can announce that such events will be filmed so everyone speaking knows they are "on the record." Organizers can also stand for democracy by providing trained facilitators who explain and enforce—and ask participants to commit to—simple rules of fair participation.

Standing for democracy means being willing to step outside our comfort zone. Let me tell you a story of my own failure to embody what I now know is required of us:

> It is the final week before the 2004 election, and I'm seated in the social hall of a synagogue in suburban Philadelphia. A debate between Lois Murphy, the candidate I've traveled here to support in her race for Congress, and the Republican incumbent, Jim Gerlach, is about to begin.
>
> The large room is overflowing, and I am eager to get my first glimpse of Gerlach, the man who had just released a message going to thousands of area telephones linking my candidate, an upstanding community member and strong advocate for women, to the Taliban!
>
> I know his ad has had an impact. The day before, as I approached one house to leave campaign literature, an agitated

man at the door asked, "Are you with the Taliban lady?" When I'd tried to explain, he threatened to unleash his angry dog.

Murphy opens by asking Gerlach to disown his dishonest ad. He refuses, no one objects, and the debate proceeds. The audience has been told to submit questions in advance but not to speak.

Only later do I realize that democracy demanded something more of me that morning.

Instead of going up to Gerlach afterward and telling him his ad was an assault on democracy—something I prided myself for doing at the time—I could have simply stood when he refused to disown his ad. I could have announced that I would remain standing until Mr. Gerlach acknowledges his mistake. My voice would have quivered as my heart pounded. But my example of respectful but firm opposition might have enabled others to stand. And even if not one person had joined me, at least there would have been an inescapable message in the room about the preciousness of the democratic principles of honesty and fair play. Beyond focusing on policy differences, everyone there would have been called to reflect on the need to defend democracy itself.

I didn't even think of doing this at the time. And if I had, my fear of embarrassment might well have stopped me. But I'm determined to become that woman, the woman who would have risen and stood, alone, if necessary.

*Speak your mind, even if your voice shakes.*

—MAGGIE KUHN

## FINDING OUR WORDS

In "getting a grip," a big piece of the challenge is disciplining ourselves to find and use words that convey a new frame, one that spreads a sense of possibility and helps people see emerging signs of Living Democracy fueling a *Spiral of Empowerment.*

I fear that, too often, terms used by those striving to live democracy fail to communicate a positive alternative to our Thin Democracy. Worse, they can be heard by others to mean the opposite of what the speaker intends.

To underscore why I believe language is so important, let me toss out a few current, deadly terms, and propose alternatives. In *Idea 5* you'll find many more examples to mull over. My goal is to get us thinking, arguing, defining and ultimately determined to stick to words that communicate what we really mean.

## ANTI-CAPITALISM OR ANTI-PLUTONOMY?

For example, in the U.S. anyone identifying "capitalism" as a root problem is likely to be understood as opposing the market system. For many Americans, any critic of capitalism must favor the only alternative they know of: a communist, state-run economy. (Worldwide, though, dissatisfaction with free market capitalism is vast. Across twenty seven countries only 11 percent of respondents polled in 2009 said they believe it "works well.")[223]

Actually, most critics of the current economic system I know are market advocates, wanting to free it from monopoly control.

So it is probably best to devise clearer terms for what we see as the problem—such as "plutonomy," the term used by Citigroup, or what I like—"a one-rule economy," which of course needs explaining. But that might be a good thing. It means an economy guided by one driver: highest return to existing wealth, which leads inexorably to monopoly.

Or one might simply name the problem as our "anti-democratic market" or America's "monopoly capitalism" that kills the market.

## GLOBALIZATION ON GLOBAL CORPORATE POWER?

To most Americans, globalization equals great Indian food, cool music from Mali, and cheap jeans from China. Economist Joseph Stiglitz in *Globalization and Its Discontents* defines globalization as "the closer integration of the countries and peoples of the world."[224]

Who in their right mind would oppose that?

Pulitzer Prize-winning columnist Thomas Friedman tells us that the current stage of globalization is "shrinking the world from size small to size tiny."[225] Distances are evaporating, he suggests. How positive! And even for those who lament the downside of outsourcing, this increasingly interconnected world is unstoppable.

But the term *globalization* focuses attention narrowly on the *scope* of activity. It diverts us from asking who is in *control* of that activity and therefore who benefits.

In other words, "globalization" jumps right over the question of power. Its defenders swoon over growing *inter*dependence—

suggesting mutuality in power relations. But the reality, propelled by one-rule economics, is deepening dependence—that is, widening power imbalances as more and more people are forced to live with the consequences of decisions made by distant boards of global corporations and by decision makers from the International Monetary Fund to the World Trade Organization, all dominated by corporate interests.

Putting the power question front and center, what if we were consistently to link the term "globalization" to centralizing corporate control?

"Corporate globalization" or "global corporate power"—both better capture what is really going on. These terms begin to alert listeners that the power of governments—of which one hundred twenty-two out of one hundred ninety-two are now elected and therefore at least nominally accountable to citizens—is giving way (or being given away) to centralizing corporate power, directed by unelected boards and managers accountable, at best, to shareholders.

And what about those movements countering global corporate power? What do we call them?

In the corporate media, they are "anti-globalization activists," which probably strikes most people as knee-jerk negative and utterly futile. But we can make clear that our vision is the essence of realism; it's globalizing corporate control that's unsustainable. So let us self-identify instead as "pro-democracy advocates." Or, even better, as "Living Democracy champions."

## FREE MARKET–FREE TRADE OR FAIR MARKET–FAIR TRADE?

Progressives often rail against "free market" policies. Wrong enemy. The free market is no more real than the tooth fairy.

"There isn't one grain of anything in the world that is sold in a free market. Not one! The only place you see a free market is in the speeches of politicians."[226] So said not an irate farmer but the CEO of agribusiness giant Archer Daniels Midland. He should know: his company and others, including Cargill and Tate & Lyle, have paid over $1 billion to settle price-fixing lawsuits.[227]

Markets are either fair or unfair; they are never "free" or "unfettered"—i.e., functioning on their own without rules. Today market rules, and there are plenty, are written to serve the interests of global corporations: The full text of the North American Free Trade Agreement runs to seventeen hundred pages. Open, fair markets result not from a "hands off" policy but from creating fair rules democratically.

As we've seen, today's one-rule economics—highest return to existing wealth, i.e., shareholders and CEOs—inexorably concentrates wealth and power, undermining competitive markets. It takes democracy—real, Living Democracy—to shape and enforce rules to keep wealth and power widely distributed—from progressive taxation to a floor under wages to anti-trust enforcement—so that markets stay fair and open. And it takes Living Democracy—citizens deliberating over shared values—to decide what should and should not be a market commodity in the first place.

So let's banish "free trade" and "free market" from our lips—unless we're prepared to redefine the latter as a market that *everyone is free to participate in* because wealth and power are generated under fair rules.

And let's clarify that it's not progressives who are anti-market. Hardly. Actually, it's the gospel of Thin Democracy that kills markets. Thin Democracy's concentration of wealth destroys competition and closes market access to all but the better off.

## REGULATIONS OR STANDARDS?

I hear "regulation," and I stiffen: I think constraint, Big Brother, red tape, inefficiency. On the other hand, most of us warm to the idea of standards; we especially love "high standards." So in addressing our needs as citizens for clean air, water and soil, for example, what if we were to substitute "standards" every time "regulation" started to pop out of our mouths?

Applied to a big 2006 step in Maine, the state didn't pass new "regulations" requiring electronics manufacturers to take responsibility for recycling TVs and computer monitors, as I discuss in Chapter 10. No. Maine raised the bar, embracing a higher standard—one in which an industry is now responsible for the lifecycle of what it produces.

Sounds really different, doesn't it?

## CONSUMERS OR BUYERS?

The very idea of "consumer" is a big handicap to thinking straight—er, I mean thinking circularly. The word "consumer" falsely conveys that what we purchase disappears from the ecosystem. But actually, we consume nothing at all. There is no "away" to which we can throw our stuff. That's the heart of what the ecological awakening teaches us, yet the word "consumer" prolongs our slumber, keeping our eyes closed to the consequences of our choices.

More accurate terms are "buyer," "purchaser," or "user." They remind us that we are simply a pass-through in a conversion process: Our "stuff" moves from extraction and processing to another state—and that state is either destructive pollution or re-use and, ultimately, healthful integration back into the wider ecosystem.

> *Words are, of course, the most powerful drug used by mankind.*
>
> —RUDYARD KIPLING[228]

## ENGAGING IN THE DIALOGUE OF DEMOCRACY

Talking democracy is, of course, not just about challenging ourselves and others to choose specific words to better convey what we mean. It is about engaging in conversation about what matters most to us—and with people holding widely diverse perspectives.

That's why I love the motto of Conversation Cafés: "Tired of small talk? Try some big talk." Check it out at conversationcafe.org. Meetup.com is another great tool through which to encounter people and explore the questions and entry points for Living Democracy.

Everyday Democracy, which opened Chapter 4, helps communities use deep dialogue to solve problems. To explore this rich world of democratic dialogue, a great place to start is the National Coalition for Dialogue and Deliberation, at thataway.org.

At this moment of assault on civil discourse, let's be really clear: We cannot get beyond band-aids to find real solutions to any of the huge problems facing our world without a functioning democracy. Grasping this, we can embed every action to move policy forward in an enlivening, inclusive, and fair process of engagement, always asking whether we are furthering the *Spiral of Empowerment*.

## Idea 5: Toward a Language of Democracy

"How forcible are right words." –Job 16:25

| WIDELY USED TERMS | CONFUSING CONNOTATIONS | ★ ALTERNATIVES TO COMMUNICATE MORE ACCURATELY & POWERFULLY ★ |
|---|---|---|
| Activist | Rabble-rouser, extremist with own agenda | • Engaged citizen<br>• Active citizen<br>• Empowered citizen |
| Anti-globalization | Backward, selfish, isolationist | • Pro-democracy<br>• Pro-strong communities<br>• Anti-corporate control<br>• Anti-economic concentration |
| Capitalism—current economic system | Often equated with positive "free market" system | • One-rule economy<br>• Plutonomy<br>• Monopoly capitalism |
| Citizenship | Burden, duty, boring | • Public engagement<br>• Community building |
| Conventional farming | Sounds benign and time-tested, when it is neither | • Chemically-dependent farming<br>• Polluting agriculture<br>• Factory farming |
| Conservatives | Implies devotion to preserving the environment and communities | • Those defending one-rule economics<br>• Anti-democratic Right (when it applies) |
| Democracy | Limited to voting and government | • Living Democracy: a way of living in which the democratic values of fairness, inclusion, and mutual accountability infuse all dimensions of our public lives. |

| | | |
|---|---|---|
| Free trade | Implies absence of government control, an automatic mechanism. It doesn't exist. | • Corporation-favoring trade<br>• Unfair trade |
| Globalization | Implies interdependence, more connection, free trade, cheaper goods | • Global corporate control<br>• Global corporatism<br>• Economic centralization<br>• Downward pressure on global wages |
| Government, as in U.S. today | Assumed to answer to citizens when it doesn't | • Privately held government<br>• Corporate-dominated government |
| Social justice | Associated with radical Left, forced equality | • Fairness<br>• Fair opportunity<br>• Freedom |
| Liberal | Favoring big government | • Progressive<br>• Favoring accountable government |
| Minimum wage | Fails to convey human impact | • Poverty wage vs. living wage |
| National debt, per person | Lacks meaning to most people | • "Birth tax"—share of nation's debt each newborn faces[123] |
| Nonprofit organization | Defined in negative | • Social Benefit Organization<br>• Citizens' organization |
| Organic farming, Low-input | Focuses only on the absence of things—synthetic pesticides and fertilizers | • Ecological farming: using the science of ecology to increase productivity and quality, while enhancing the environment<br>• Knowledge-intensive farming |
| Pro-choice | Sounds trivial | • Pro-conscience* |

| | | |
|---|---|---|
| Pro-life | Misleads: making abortion illegal doesn't lessen it. | • For criminalizing abortion |
| Protest, demonstration | Limited, defensive | • "Civic obedience"– a positive act to defend democratic values |
| Public life | Restricted to officials and celebrities | • What we each do as buyer, worker, employer, parent, voter, investor, and in all the other roles we play daily making huge ripples |
| Regulation | Big Brother, top-down intrusive government, inefficiency | • Standards protecting ownership diversity, competition, health, and the environment<br>• Public protections; "values boundaries" within which the market serves community |
| Right to same-sex marriage | Focuses on sexuality | • Freedom to marry<br>• Equal marriage |
| Taxes | Burden, rip-off of "our" money | • Membership dues for a strong, healthy society<br>• "The price of civilization," as Justice Oliver Wendell Holmes, Jr., put it |
| Welfare state | Coddling people, big bureaucracy | • Fair-opportunity state |

*My gratitude to Kathleen Kennedy Townsend for this term, which she reports was suggested by a nun.

# PART 3
# COURAGE

# 8 SEIZE THE MOMENT

*In 1974 I would walk by people dying from famine to teach my economics class at the university...and I said: "What is this?" I felt completely empty.... The theories I was teaching were useless for these dying people. I realized I could help people as a human being, not as an economist. So I decided to become a basic human being.... I no longer carried any pre-conceived notions.*

—DR. MUHAMMAD YUNUS, 2006 NOBEL PEACE PRIZE LAUREATE & FOUNDER OF GRAMEEN BANK, BANGLADESH[229]

We humans see pretty much what we expect to see, I've argued. We often can't even register what doesn't fit our picture of how the world works.

Yikes. "If that's true," you may well respond, "how is it possible ever to change? Aren't we frozen in self-destruct mode?"

No, I don't think so. I've witnessed people doing the apparently impossible—perceiving the "screen" through which they now peer, seeing with new eyes, then moving forward with improved vision.

It's hard, but sometimes we get lucky. We get a kick in the pants. We experience a moment of internal dissonance in which we suddenly realize that our old ways of seeing no longer helps us make sense of our world.

As I write this, I sense that literally millions of Americans may well be having such luck. Having thrown themselves into President

Obama's campaign, tearfully celebrating on election night 2008, many now feel disoriented. *What happened?* Their hero entrusted our collapsing economy to the very people—including Timothy Geithner and Ben Bernanke—whose decisions over many years had brought us to disaster. His Afghanistan buildup appears little different from what George W. Bush might have chosen.

The ground shakes. One is forced to look more deeply. To look at the underlying forces that having a new leader in the White House did not seem to change.

## TRAPPED AND SPRINGING FREE

This book suggests that many of us are trapped in the *Spiral of Powerlessness* you can find inside the front cover. It suggests that our materialistic, competitive culture denies deep needs that live within virtually all of us. (Perhaps one sign is that more than half of us are unhappy with our work.)[230] Many of us learn to deny that we're squelching such needs—needs for cooperation and efficacy and fairness. Maybe it is just too painful to acknowledge how much of ourselves we're giving up. But if these needs aren't met, most of us don't just roll over and pretend we don't have them; we seek their satisfaction in less-than-ideal ways—moving us into the *cycle of fear*, in the lower half of *Idea 6*.

Unable to satisfy our yearning for connection through common endeavor, we try the next best thing—feeling included because of our outer identities: wearing what's "in" or choosing work we think will please our parents or bring us status.

Our yearning for power gets twisted, too. Power, as I've said, means our "capacity to act." But if we feel we can't make a dent positively, we go for control. If we feel put down at work or at home, not heard or seen, we're tempted to try to exert control over something—maybe our child, our spouse. In its extreme form, the response to thwarting our innate need for power is violence.

Psychiatrist and author James Gilligan has spent much of his long career working with violent criminals. He stresses the deep human need for acceptance and power, then tells us violence is sometimes the only avenue to respect that the men he treats see as available to them. He quotes a violent inmate in a running battle with correction officers: "...I've got to have my self-respect, and I've declared war on the whole world till I get it!"[231]

But not only do ersatz avenues for getting what we want fail to satisfy, they make things worse. Addictive eating can destroy our bodies, addictive shopping destroys our ecosystem and attempts to control others creates resistance and fear.

A vicious cycle moves into high gear as we strive harder, causing the gap between our inner needs and the reality outside to expand into a chasm. The bigger it gets, the more we cling to our ways, for at least they're familiar.

No wonder it can seem impossible to break free of this destructive cycle.

## IDEA 6: Inner World of Living Democracy

**Experience Joy**
in truer connection & greater efficacy

**Ease Fear**
by attracting and embracing new "tribes"

**Glimpse Possibility**
of more life-serving mental maps and follow curiosity

**Find Entry Points**
to act personally to shift causal patterns towards life

Cycle of **HOPE**

**Recognize Fear**
as a call to courage, not a verdict of failure

**MOMENT OF DISSONANCE/ MOMENT OF OPPORTUNITY**

How do I respond?

We become conscious of the disconnect between our inner needs and the outer world. Our mental map cracks. Fear of expulsion from the "tribe" arises.

**Experience Fear**
of acting on our need to create a world truer to our values

Cycle of **FEAR**

**Feel Disconnect**
between inner sense of fairness & empathy and the "real" world

**Deny**
our need for connection & efficacy and deny our denial!

**Crises Worsen**
citizens disengage; society & environment degrade further

**Seek Substitutes**
connection via consumption; efficacy via control & violence

Concepts explored in *Hope's Edge* (2002), *You Have the Power* (2004) and *Democracy's Edge* (2006). Adapted by Frances Moore Lappé and Richard Rowe, Small Planet Institute, www.smallplanet.org.

## A RUDE SHOCK

Sometimes, though, we get a big helper—what Bangladeshi Muhammad Yunus, quoted above, calls a "rude shock." His happened in the early 1970s after Yunus had returned to his starving, war-ravaged country to teach following a stint in a Tennessee university. His shock came the moment he admitted to himself that his classroom theories weren't helping, and might even be hurting.

"Seize the moment" typically refers to a positive moment of opportunity, one not to be wasted. Gradually it's dawned on me, though, that such a moment can come as a disconcerting shock, dissonance that might not feel too good at the time. It is in these precious moments—when something shakes us up, rattling us from our resignation or depression, or galvanizing that vague sense that there must be more to life—that we can break free of the *cycle of fear*.

Dr. Yunus's moment of dissonance led him to drop his textbook theories and begin to listen to poor people themselves. He learned that their poverty was linked to their virtual servitude to money lenders, and his "aha" was the realization that credit on fair terms, unavailable to poor people, could transform their lives. Bankers laughed at him. But Yunus moved into the *cycle of hope*, and his moment of dissonance led to an international microcredit movement that's since expanded to sixty countries, lifting tens of millions of people out of poverty.

And to a Nobel Peace Prize for Dr. Yunus.

One early moment of dissonance for me occurred as I was sitting in the UC Berkeley agricultural library at age twenty-six, astounded that evidence of world food abundance clashed with headlines and textbooks, all warning of impending food shortages. I wanted to shout to the world: "Nature doesn't make hunger. Humans do!"

I felt like the little boy in the fairy tale who says the emperor wears no clothes. I was scared, really scared—what if I'd misplaced a decimal point and gotten it all wrong? How could I be right and the grown-up "experts" mistaken?

But I couldn't turn back. I couldn't stay quiet.

Fortunately, we don't have to rely on accidental encounters to trigger these precious moments. We can each expose ourselves to people, ideas, and events that create internal dissonance—that feeling that something just doesn't fit right anymore.

I think, for example, of a couple who, in the fall of 2006, approached me to sign a book for their young daughter. We were gathered in the anteroom of a gorgeous Pittsburgh hotel ballroom after celebrating the work of a local social-benefit organization called Just Harvest, as well as that of the United Steel Workers.

A bit timidly at first, they told me they'd always felt comfortable as Republicans within a "conservative" Christian church, but earlier in the year a light had gone on for them: They had exposed themselves to new ideas and suddenly realized that the Bush administration had not leveled with Americans about Iraq and had led us into disaster there. With heavy hearts they shared their new perspective with their minister, himself a staunch defender of the administration.

The minister sternly warned the couple: "Don't tell anyone else in the church, because they will turn against you." This "rude shock" jolted the couple out of a place of comfort. They had to choose, and they chose to engage with new ideas, new people.

As I listened, I felt emboldened by their courage and joyful that we were together that night, celebrating a group addressing the roots of hunger, a group their church might have considered subversive. This family experienced the dissonance at the center of the Inner World of Living Democracy, *Idea 6*, then broke away from a limiting frame and became free to discover new "tribes." Their discovery eased the pain of separation and encouraged them to continue to listen to their conscience.

In moments such as the ones this young family experienced, we each choose. Do we suppress the discomfort? Or do we listen to it and delve into the disconnect, making the leap necessary to put the world together in a new way, the essence of the *cycle of hope*?

## LETTING GO OF ILLUSIONS

Feelings of disorientation, deflation and confusion are all totally understandable in today's world. But if this book's thesis holds water, then illusion is our real enemy. And what a chance to let it go! The illusion of many Americans in 2008, for example, that changing a leader could yield significantly better results without changing the rules—including those governing *how* we choose leaders—is dangerous. Only if we let it go can we get on with the work, the real work of living democracy.

To be sure, these are not once-in-a-lifetime moments. We'll have, if we're lucky, many such moments during which we have to listen to our inner wisdom, question our path, and see with new eyes. Our hearts may be torn open. It may hurt, or it may be thrilling. But we know we'll never be the same.

# 9 WHEN FEAR MEANS GO

*The danger lies in refusing to face the fear...courage is more exhilarating than fear, and in the long run it is easier.*

—ELEANOR ROOSEVELT[232]

In these moments of dissonance, fear can always stop us dead in our tracks, for it has become the "emotional plague of our planet," observes French philosopher Patrick Viveret.

To break free, we must understand how we arrived here, and to do that, we have to reach back in time. Way back.

Evolving eons ago within tightly knit tribes smack dab among species bigger and fiercer than us, we learned one lesson well: Alone, we don't stand a chance. So banishment meant sure death.

Humans are hardwired through eons of evolutionary experience to sense that our survival depends on staying on the "inside"—with the tribe. It shouldn't surprise us that scientists now report that our bodies experience the pain of being rejected as we do actual physical pain. We thrive on the approval of others; we dread humiliation above all else.

So it's hard for human beings to say, "No, the whole pack is heading toward catastrophe!" We fear being cast out. So we hold back.

Yet our world's hyper-tribe *is* about to paddle over Victoria Falls—fouling air and water, speeding wealth's concentration, and building more and more weapons of mass destruction. In this situation, breaking from the pack means life.

Yet it *still* brings up instinctual fear.

Remember, though, that fear is in part an *idea*, and we know that ideas can trump instinct. Don't believe me? Consider "honor killings," in which fathers become murderers of daughters. Here an idea obviously trumps a primal instinct—parents' protection of offspring.

Back to the positive: we can remake the idea of fear itself and reshape our instinctual responses. Based on my own experience and on hard science, I have come to believe that despite our biological heritage, we can *choose* how we respond to fear.

This may in fact be the most important choice of our lives.

We can learn to reinterpret fear not as a verdict but as a signal. Whereas eons ago, breaking with the pack meant death, perhaps in today's circumstances it means just the opposite—it may be the only path to life.

With this insight, we can come to interpret our own body's fear sensations anew: Maybe they are not telling us that we're off track but that we are precisely where we should be—at our growth edge. We can see fear as pure energy, a tool we can work with.

## FEAR AS PURE ENERGY

This possibility and the momentous consequences of this shift came to me one night in Nairobi, Kenya, as my daughter Anna and I recount in *Hope's Edge*. There we met the Reverend Timothy Njoya, who had done something which until that evening I believed no human being could do.

For preaching a pro-democracy message despite the repeated threats against him by a dictatorial government, seven armed assailants appeared one night at his door. Despite all he'd been through, Reverend Njoya—a slight and agile man—playfully acted out for us what happened next. As he described his fingers being sliced off, his belly slashed open, he was chuckling!

...Me? My heart was beating wildly in my chest.

Then he told us that, as he lay on the floor, certain he was dying, he began to give his treasures away to his attackers—to one, his favorite Bible, to another, his library, and so on.

*What!?* I thought to myself. *How can this be? How could anyone not respond with sheer terror and life-preserving aggression to such brutality?*

So I asked: "But...Reverend Njoya, how were you not overcome by fear?"

Sitting deep in the cushioned armchair, his sweet face framed by a stiff white priest's collar, Reverend Njoya paused for only a moment. Then he said, "Fear is an energy that comes from inside us, not outside. It's neutral. So we can channel it into fear, paranoia, or euphoria, whatever we choose." He rose out of his chair.

"Imagine a lion," he said, crouching. "When a lion sees prey or predator, it senses fear first. But instead of lunging blindly in defense or in attack, it recoils." Reverend Njoya moved back, leaning on his left leg and crouching lower. "The lion pauses a moment, targets his energies. Then he springs."

"We can do the same. We can harness our would-be fears, harmonize our energies, and channel them into courage." His whole body, his whole life, seemed to tell us, yes, this is possible. Reverend Njoya's response—that of generosity in the face of brutality—so moved his assailants that it was they who rushed him to the hospital where doctors saved him.

Reverend Njoya's ability to re-channel the energy of his fear saved his life.

Anna and I lay awake in our guest house bunks talking well into the night, and since then I've reflected many times on Reverend Njoya's story. I've learned that I don't have to pray that my fear will—finally, finally—go away and leave me alone. Nor do I have to reach Reverend Njoya's level of self-mastery in order to recognize that, yes, fear is within me, not in an external force. I can harness the energy of fear and, like the lion taking aim, choose where and what I do with it.

## FEAR AND CONFLICT

As fear spreads throughout our culture, it's not surprising that many of us are even more tempted to run from conflict—to duck for cover, as the previous chapter explores. "In times of danger," writes Rush Dozier in *Fear Itself*, "when there is no immediate avenue of escape, [our brain's] primitive fear system tries to shut off any unnecessary movement, reasoning that if you stay still you might not be noticed."[233]

Not crossing anyone, we stay under the radar, or at least that's the hope of the primitive brain. Imagine the rabbit frozen motionless in the grass.

Willie Manteris, fifty-three, whom I met in 2003 in an airport coffee shop far from home, told me that, in effect, he'd been that rabbit most of his life. Willie had achieved his dream—a successful dentistry practice in a Pittsburgh suburb, a big home on Club House Drive, two bright children, and a wife with a prestigious job. "In my family growing up, conflict was terrifying, destructive, and upsetting—something to be avoided at all costs," Willie told me, as we sat chatting in Porto Alegre, Brazil. "I had built my whole life by making no waves; conflict was the worst taboo, the worst fear."

But since Willie and I were both on our way home from the World Social Forum, the largest gathering anywhere of citizens trying as hard as they could to make waves, something obviously had changed for Willie.

Three years earlier, Willie had sold his dentistry practice to follow his heart. "The biggest fear and the most powerful was the hidden and invisible one: It was stepping out of the conformity and anonymity, stepping out of old roles in which I felt safe and comfortable. It meant defining the self: who I really was, who I was in the world. It meant risking conflict."

And Willie did, as he began traveling regularly to Central America with Pastors for Peace, offering both material supplies and challenging widespread abuses of indigenous people's rights.

"One of the prices you pay for staying trapped by that fear is that you don't learn how to express healthy dissent. Stepping out of those shadows and voicing oneself is too scary. Politically, it put me for most of my life in a role of being submissive and passive," Willie said.

The consequences of staying stuck in conflict aversion, as Willie had been, are momentous. Fear of conflict too often keeps good people silent, blocking us from participating as the full-voiced citizens of a real democracy we could be.

Even more worrisome, if we fear we can't handle conflict ourselves, we may be tempted to choose authoritarian, "strongman" leaders. In taking us to war in Iraq, I noticed that George W. Bush typically spoke about what "I" the president will do, but rarely about what we as citizens could do. His approach reinforced feelings of helplessness, of the sense that all we can do is put our fate in his hands.

As long as we don't feel we have what it takes to face conflict, do we unconsciously hope authoritarians will squash conflict for us? Burmese Nobel Peace Laureate Aung San Suu Kyi—who, for her pro-democracy heroism, has been brutalized by the military elite and held under house arrest for years, and is still in detention—shares this worry:

"It is not power that corrupts, but fear," Suu Kyi writes in *Freedom from Fear*. "Fear of losing power corrupts those who wield it and fear of the scourge of power corrupts those who are subject to it."[234]

## AS IT IS

I believe Aung San Suu Kyi is talking about not just the fear of confronting brutal dictators but an even wider fear of standing up to bullying. Mostly, the fear is psychological. Lab studies show that many of us go along with the majority, even when we *know* the majority is wrong and all that's at stake is the risk of being out of step. Rather than buck an official-looking authority, more than six out of ten of us, disturbing studies show, will obey even when it means inflicting pain on others.[235]

I love focusing on evidence that positive human qualities enabling us to "live democracy"—including the basic need for fairness and the capacity for empathy—are virtually universal. But I also believe the word "virtually" in that sentence needs our attention.

Both my own life experience and psychiatric experts tell me that, mainly due to being brutalized as youngsters, a tiny minority of people are deficient in the empathetic sensibilities—i.e., the conscience—that almost all of us take for granted. In fact, it's *because* these sensibilities are so widespread that many people have difficulty acknowledging they might be missing in a few.[236] At the extreme, I have witnessed this dysfunction show up in lying without guilt, hurting without remorse, and intimidating with satisfaction.

> *The want or imperfection of a moral sense in some men, like the want or imperfection of the senses of sight and hearing in others, is no proof that it is a general characteristic of the species.*
>
> —THOMAS JEFFERSON, 1814[237]

And why bring up this sad point? The last thing I want to do is heighten the mistrust spread by our dominant culture's frame. But I also know we can't heal our planet unless we perceive life as it is, not as we wish it to be.

I think of what I'm striving for as *heart-centered realism.*

It includes gaining strength to "walk with our fear" of conflict so that we can name harmful dysfunction and rally ourselves and others to effectively contain its damage. Groups taking seriously the notion that democracy is, at its root, about "how we treat one another" deliberately spell out standards of interaction to which members commit because they've helped choose them. The commitments often include respectful listening and constructive feedback, essential to the democratic arts in Chapter 6.

Making such commitments explicit provides protection: clear boundaries the group can enforce, if necessary, so the destructiveness of a tiny minority need not upend the good work of many.[238]

Heart-centered realism means gaining the tools—including rethinking fear—to stand up to bullying, whether within our own house or the White House. It means gaining the confidence to stand up to "group think," as, for example, when in 2002 and early 2003 the Bush White House used false evidence—and admonished those who questioned it—regarding Iraq's threat in order to persuade Americans to back the administration's longstanding intent to invade. Almost all the nation's major media went along—with the striking exception of two Knight Ridder (now McClatchy) news service journalists, Jonathan Landay and Warren Strobel, who dug for the facts and stood by them—despite their admitted queasiness about being out of step.[239]

Our culture doesn't prepare us for such bravery—on which Living Democracy depends—but psychologist Martha Stout of Harvard Medical School offers commonsense advice:

"Trust your own instincts and anxieties, especially those concerning people who claim that dominating others, violence, war, or some other violation of your conscience is the grand solution," she writes. "Do this even when, or especially when, everyone around you has completely stopped questioning authority..." Note that in lab experiments on human complicity in brutality, when even a few people resist, others join them.[240]

Living Democracy demands that we ask ourselves: Even if a tiny minority suffers an empathy deficit, can we in good conscience blame them? *Their power to harm is always inversely proportional to the courage exhibited by others who are, after all, the majority.*

Maybe this realization is what it really means to grow up as a species.

And it means we must rethink fear itself so that we can see what some others may not want to see and say what they may not want to hear.

## OLD THOUGHTS, NEW THOUGHTS

It is an extraordinary era: We alive today may be the first in human evolution able to look at how our biology serves us—or does not serve us—and then choose: We can respond in old, programmed ways—flee, fight, freeze—or we can know fear simply as information. It may well be information showing that we're pushing our growth edge, making fear's energy now available for creative ends.

> *We are to learn about fear, not how to escape from it.*
>
> —JIDDU KRISHNAMURTI

Instead of robbing us of power, I came to see fear as a resource we use to create the world we want. I've always imagined Reverend Njoya's attackers as seven swordsmen at his door, and now I realize that, like him, we each will meet our seven swordsmen. Only for us, they are our culture's dangerous ideas about fear. *Idea 7* contrasts seven limiting thoughts about fear that I've experienced and seven new, freeing ones.

Each of these ideas frames a chapter in *You Have the Power: Choosing Courage in a Culture of Fear*, which Jeffrey Perkins and I wrote together.

I now believe that, like Reverend Njoya, we can transform these assailants into that which can save us.

## INNER APPLAUSE

Indeed, the future of life on our beleaguered planet may hinge on such mental jujitsu. Can we learn to transform fear by reinterpreting its meaning? The pounding heart, the tight throat, the weak knees…all may mean we're doing exactly what our truer selves most want in that moment.

I recall sitting in an audience after Al Gore presented the Boston debut of *An Inconvenient Truth.* I was moved by the film; yet I was alarmed, too. Why didn't his prescription for solutions match the magnitude of global climate chaos? Why didn't he emphasize the essential step: removing the power of concentrated wealth from our political decision making?

As soon as the question popped into my head, my heart started to pound. Because other questioners were showering Gore with praise, I realized I'd be out of sync if I were to speak up. Then something new happened. As soon as I became aware of the thump-thump-thump in my chest, I knew I *had* to raise my hand.

My body was telling me something—not that I was a wimp, but that what I had to say was important. That's when I realized I could choose to reinterpret my pounding heart as secret "inner applause" telling me that I'm really exactly where I should be.

By the way, Al Gore never did call on me that night...but I left partially satisfied, anyway, knowing that I didn't shrink back.

So let us expose as myth the notion of "getting over fear." In being true to ourselves, we will always risk separation, and separation will always be frightening. But we can each learn to walk ever taller with our fear, as we lead the way toward life.

## Idea 7: Seven Ways to Rethink Fear

| | OLD THOUGHTS | NEW THOUGHTS |
|---|---|---|
| 1 | Fear means I'm in danger. Something's wrong. I must escape and seek safety. | Fear is pure energy. It's a signal. It might not mean stop, it could mean go! |
| 2 | If I stop what I'm doing, I'll be lost. I'll never start again. | Sometimes we have to stop in order to find our path. |
| 3 | I have to figure it all out before I can do anything. | We don't have to believe we can do it to do it; the decision to act itself has power. |
| 4 | If I act on what I believe, conflict will break out. I'll be humiliated, ineffective, and rejected. | Conflict means engagement. Something real is in motion. It's an opening, not a closing. |
| 5 | Our greatest fears are our worst enemies; they drag us down and hold us back. | Our worst fears can be our greatest teachers. |
| 6 | If I'm really myself, I'll be excluded. If I break connection, I'll be alone forever. | To find genuine connection, we must risk disconnection. The new light we shine draws others toward us, and we become conscious choosers. |
| 7 | I'm just a drop in the bucket. My effort might make me feel better, but it can't do much. | Every time we act, even with fear, we make room for others to do the same. Courage is contagious. |

From *You Have the Power: Choosing Courage in a Culture of Fear* by Frances Moore Lappé and Jeffrey Perkins, Tarcher/Penguin 2004.

# 10 SANITY IN MOTION

*It is far too late and things are far too bad for pessimism.*

—DEE HOCK, FOUNDER OF VISA[241]

If Dee Hock got it right, how *do* we escape pessimism? Not so that we can settle into blind optimism, putting on a smiley face to block out the suffering–especially our own.

Rather, I see the challenge this way, "How do we escape paralysis by becoming 'possibilists,' living daily with a renewed and renewing sense of possibility that enables us to become ever more fully awake?"

That's what I want.

One thing's for sure: I know I'm not going to get there, or to any new place, if I keep on going where I've always gone. You've probably heard my favorite definition of insanity—it's been around a long time: doing the very same thing over and over again and expecting it to turn out differently. (The idea has been attributed to both Benjamin Franklin and Albert Einstein.)

Hearing it, I always smile inside, for I have to admit falling prey myself to this grand delusion. Maybe we all have. But on the most crucial questions of our time, neither humanity nor the earth itself can any longer survive our refusal to learn.

So I've titled this final chapter "sanity in motion" because that's what's required—that we claim our sanity as we choose to act. But to stop repeating the "same-olds" and live in a state of possibility, we need at least three things:

As you now know, I believe, first we need a good working theory of how we got here and, second, a belief in the possibility of deep change. Third, we need points of entry that interrupt and shift the pattern that got us into this horrific mess.

## REMEMBERING HOW WE GOT HERE

Let me recount for you, with a few new twists, the realizations I've come to as I've attempted, for my own sanity, to peel away layers of causation.

Under its front cover, this book begins with the dangerously false premise in the center of it all: that there isn't *enough*. There aren't enough goods, nor is there enough goodness.

And now some tell us that time itself is lacking. We have no time to draw people into solution-making and build democratic skills and communities; the planet is on the ropes. Top-down strategies are efficient, we still hear, even though they got us into this mess to begin with and suppress precisely the networks of creativity and commitment on which real solutions depend. We have no time for democracy, we're still told, even though it's inconceivable that we can make right our relationship to the earth without making right our relationships with one another.

But the most debilitating piece of the scarcity message is its insistence on the lack inside us. A constricted self-concept drives the dominant worldview, reinforced not only by dominant political and economic theory, not only by incessant corporate advertising, but also by strains within many religions. The first two reduce us to competitive accumulators; the third may be even worse—emphazing that we are unclean sinners. (Note, though, that the doctrine of "original sin" didn't appear until the 4th century).

From this premise of lack, we *are* finished. We end up locked in a belief system that actually creates the very scarcity we fear.

With this dim view of ourselves, we're vulnerable to simplistic social dogma—to grand "isms" encouraging us to turn over our fate to infallible laws, such as the mythical "free market;" and to distant institutions, such as the formal trappings of democracy—not to mention dictators and ayatollahs.

Here in the West, where market dogma holds many spellbound, we allow a one-rule economy to take hold (economic life driven by highest return to existing wealth) that inevitably concentrates money and decision making in the hands of a tiny minority. This concentration kills precisely what we say we hold quite dear—a competitive market and political decision making accountable to the public good.

Our planet's survival therefore depends on whether we can break free—whether we can affirm not the goodness *of* human nature, as I've stressed, but the richness *in* human nature.

Nature, it turns out, has equipped us with just what we need to make this great turning: our soft-wired needs and capacities for community bonding, for meaning and efficacy beyond day-to-day survival, and for fairness. We are also profoundly creative, learning creatures. "Fortunately, the human brain comes equipped with a very special feature," writes radiology and psychiatry professor Andrew Newberg. "It can alter its system of beliefs far more rapidly than that of any other organism on the planet."

## SEEING PATTERN, I CAN BEGIN

Even when a task seems monumental—cleaning out the attic or writing a book—I do find the energy to tackle it, *if* I can see the first steps. *If* I can see how a small action—getting together a few boxes or creating a one-page outline—connects to my ultimate goal: an attic where I can actually find things, or a book that might help us find answers.

But to take part in the birth of the new also requires, as I noted in this book's opening pages, that we let go of a central, ego-satisfying myth: that our challenge is ridding the world of the evil other, certain we ourselves are incapable of the inhumanity we see in them. At the dawn of the twenty-first century, evidence defies this ego-salving prescription. The Holocaust, Rwanda, Hiroshima, and so many more atrocities all involved acts by "normal people" who inflicted suffering and death on innocents.

Understandably, human beings have resisted the painful admission of our own potential for evil, but there's a huge reward awaiting us, if we can drop our resistance.

Freed from the idea that our misery is caused by an incurably evil "other," we are able to ask: *Okay, what exactly are the conditions under which brutality will almost certainly surface?* The premise of this book has been that, if we can identify with some confidence the conditions that bring out the worst in us, we know what to do: We address precisely those conditions.

Fortunately, social psychologists and cultural historians tell us they are not so difficult to discern. In Chapter 1, I land on three: *extreme imbalances in power* that thwart the creative energies of the disempowered and distort the humanity of the powerful; *anonymity* that shields us from accountability and distances us from our innate connection and caring; and *scapegoating* through which we deny responsibility ourselves while pushing blame elsewhere, even to the point of dehumanizing others.

These conditions create a culture of fear and rigid thinking, which we know causes most of us to shut down and to see others as potential threats.

Getting clear on what calls forth our darker side gives us power to create the world we want. It enables us to choose specific values and practices, such as those sketched throughout this book, that can dissolve *each* of these abuse-generating conditions. In other words, as we make democracy a way of life, we are:

- **continually dispersing power**—building decision-making structures of mutual accountability and nurturing the skills to hold accountable those in positions of greater authority.
- **dissolving anonymity**—enhancing community bonds and establishing transparency, from school board meetings to Wall Street practices.
- **lessening the likelihood of stereotyping and scapegoating**—insisting on inclusion by linking diverse people and building democratic communication skills, from listening to creative conflict.

Each of the stories in this book contributes to creating one or more of these three assets of Living Democracy, and we each can be part of furthering them.

How to begin?

## A CAUTIONARY TALE: THE DANGER OF GOOD INTENTIONS

Before answering directly, let me share a cautionary tale from the 1970s. Joe Collins and I, both barely thirty years old, had just met through our common outrage over world hunger, which for the first time had hit the international marquee. We were determined to create an institute (ultimately becoming the Institute for Food and Development Policy, a.k.a. Food First) with a strong voice helping to find solutions.

We heard most public voices, especially those within religious communities, calling for food aid—shipping our food at low or no cost to hungry nations—as the moral response: We have so much and they have so little, so let's transfer some of our bounteous supply to them. American farmers felt heroic as they responded to the call.

On the surface, who could argue? The simple logic moved hearts.

But Joe and I, burying ourselves in research about the hungriest places on earth, learned startling facts: Many of these nations produced enough for all to eat, but many of their people were too poor to buy it. Moreover, we discovered that chronically importing subsidized food can undercut local farmers, depriving them of markets, and shifting tastes away from locally grown foods—all making future food self-reliance more difficult.

Yes, providing short-term food aid to poor countries is absolutely essential to saving lives in emergencies, but food in most cases can be bought within the region, thus benefiting poor farmers nearby. But U.S. agribusiness has been able to block this commonsense approach and cause deadly delays in famine relief by insisting that our government use only U.S. suppliers.[242] Only in recent years, through tremendous citizen pressure, has the practice begun to change.[243]

So "U.S. food aid" became my own personal code words for, "Good intentions aren't enough. They can even backfire!" They can backfire if they are blind to underlying patterns of disempowerment at the root of the suffering.

## CHANGING COURSE—ISSUES VERSUS ENTRY POINTS

It helps me to think both "big picture" and "specific action" at once. To be motivated, I need to know how a specific step avoids "insanity"—that is, repeating the old while expecting the new. I need to see how it helps us change course.

To avoid the unintended backfiring of "helpful" acts, we can keep asking, "How am I interrupting a negative cycle that creates suffering or reinforcing a positive one that helps create the conditions we know bring forth the best in us?" To answer that question, I find it helpful to distinguish between "issues" and "entry points."

"Issues" overwhelm. They hit us as distinct problems, piles and piles of them. We hear of child slavery, violence against women, hunger, HIV/AIDS, deepening inequality, pollution and global heating, failing schools...

Yikes. I feel buried, smothered under a mountain of problems. I want to cry "Uncle!"

"Entry points" are very different.

We can detect an entry point if we're weaving a theory of causation, so that we can pinpoint places to start shifting the killer cycle itself. Entry points break into and deflect the *Spiral of Powerlessness* presented inside the front cover. They are deliberate actions that speed a new directional flow of causation, fueling the *Spiral of Empowerment* presented inside the back cover.

To fully manifest our power, we can come to see how specific entry points available to us right now actually help us change course. So I've grouped some entry points within what I call "course changers"—three big shifts that cut deeply, deeply enough not only to pull us back from the brink but to redirect us toward life-giving societies. Course changers shift us from

*. . . a magical-monopoly market to a democratic market*

*. . . a culture of victims and blamers to a culture of empowerment and mutuality*

*. . . a politics driven by money to a politics driven by citizens' values*

Seeing the possibility of changing course, we realize we can have the society we want: health care, for example, equal to the best in the world, instead of an embarrassing thirty-seventh; an education system worthy of our people, instead of one in which our children fall behind twenty-four other countries in math; and an economy in which we're all advancing but the poorest are making the most progress, as we experienced from the 1940s to the 1970s.[244]

Within each "course changer" are many, many entry points. But here I'll include just a few—bare glimpses of what is underway but currently out of sight. So, none is a pipedream; even within a one-rule economy of Thin Democracy, all are beginning. If we're honest with ourselves, though, we know that they can only cascade into trend-altering power as we reclaim democratic decision making from private control at every level.

So here goes.

## COURSE CHANGER 1: *FROM MAGICAL-MONOPOLY MARKET TO DEMOCRATIC MARKET*

I've made a big deal in this book about letting go of the failed notion that the market works on its own to serve us. No, I've said, it needs us; for on its own, without the guidance of citizens able to set values-boundaries, the market concentrates power, killing what we love. So here are a couple of entry points in which citizens, through their governing bodies and directly through their choices, are shaping the market to serve life.

### Entry point 1 Citizen to producer: "You made it, you're responsible."

An "issue" is mountains of electronic waste, much of it toxic, clogging landfills, as well as the planet-heating burning of fossil fuels used to manufacture millions of new electronic gadgets every year—in part because so few get recycled.

Making a PC monitor, it turns out, uses ten times its weight in fossil fuels, while cars and refrigerators use between one and two times their weight. So the annual global manufacturing of nearly 300 million computers contributes to both the spread of toxic chemicals and global heating.[245]

One way to confront this issue would be to enact stricter rules about what consumers must do with obsolete electronics. But...an entry point? An entry point shifts the inner logic of the problem. It places the market within a framework of values driven by empowered citizens. A truly "democratic market."

And it's what Maine citizens began to experience in early 2006 when their new "producer responsibility" law went into effect: It requires that producers putting certain electronic products into our world also carry responsibility for their lifecycle, including the cost of recycling.

Suddenly, with that one shift, producers are motivated to make less toxic and more recyclable things. And less fossil fuel is used because there's less manufacturing from scratch.

"It's too wasteful to try to retrofit after things are built. We don't have time. We have to build sustainability into products," Pete Didisheim told me. He is the advocacy director for the Natural Resources Council of Maine, a group that led a campaign making Maine the first U.S. state to enact "producer responsibility" laws.

For Pete, it was a shocking video, *Exporting Harm*, that lit the "producer responsibility" fire in his belly. He saw unprotected Chinese workers dismantling discarded computers from the industrial countries, unknowingly exposing themselves to deadly lead, cadmium, and other toxins.

"This is the dark side of our information age," he told me.

So he, along with the Maine environmental council, got busy and found legislative sponsors (including a Republican landfill operator who had seen the problem close up) to introduce a bill to get to the root of the crisis.

Before the bill's passage, each year Mainers threw out an estimated one hundred thousand computers and televisions, each with an array of toxic materials inside, including deadly mercury and three to eight pounds of toxic lead. Because much waste in Maine is incinerated, a lot of harmful fumes were polluting this breathtaking state.

Since 2006, because of the bill, manufacturers pick up most of the cost of dismantling and recycling TVs and computer monitors. Consumers are required to take televisions and monitors to a transfer station; from there they go to state-approved centers that recycle them and bill manufacturers for the cost—as much as forty-eight cents a pound.

During the first two years under the new rules, more than eight million pounds of electronic waste—about seven pounds per Mainer—were collected, preventing as much as 1.5 million pounds of lead, plus significant amounts of other toxins, from entering Maine's landfills and incinerators. That's over a pound of lead avoided for every citizen of the state![246]

By 2009, twenty other states had passed producer responsibility laws and twelve more are considering the approach.[247] It's being used in twenty-nine countries as well.

Do you think that when Pete watched that shocking movie and decided to act he could have imagined the speed with which this commonsense strategy would spread?

### Entry point 2 New rules reward and spread decentralized, renewable energy production.

An urgent "issue" is global heating from fossil fuel, the danger of nuclear power, and the need for non-polluting, non-planet-heating, safe, renewable energy sources. But where's the entry point in a global economy dominated by a trillion-dollar-plus oil industry?

Many people devoting their lives to getting us off fossil fuel and nuclear power hail one, simple, win-win set of rules. Already speeding the use of renewable energy technologies in over sixty countries, states, provinces, and territories, the strategy goes by the name "feed-in tariff," with the great acronym FIT. Germany and Spain are leading the way.

The law simply obligates utilities to buy electricity from renewable installations at a price carefully calculated to ensure reasonable profits. Green energy producers are thus guaranteed a good market, reducing investment risk to virtually zero. Households, communities, and farmers are invited in on the act—it is open to all.

As billions in public subsidies now go to benefit the fossil fuel and nuclear industries, feed-in laws begin to correct the grossly tilted playing field.

In Germany, costs are spread among all bill-paying households, so the law adds only around €3 ($4.00) a month for each, in return for around 300,000 jobs and a world-class industry worth billions to the country's economy.

In southern Germany, the seven hundred people of the village of Jühnde demonstrate the law's potential. All its energy now comes from renewable sources, including farm wastes, according to Miguel Mendonça, who's written two definitive books on the approach: *Feed-in Tariffs* and *Powering the Green Economy—The Feed-in Tariff Handbook*.[248]

Miguel told me of big "solar parks" in Spain, one hour's drive from Pamplona, next to a village called Milagro: "They have one of Europe's biggest—the size of fifty football pitches [soccer fields]—with arrays of huge solar photovoltaic panels."

This solar park, with roughly seven hundred fifty owners, is run cooperatively—as is more and more common. "There are plenty of enthusiastic investors," says Miguel, because "a tax break reduces the investment and the feed-in tariff brings a guaranteed annual income." Milagro's mayor Esteban Garijo thinks it's a brilliant idea: "The sun doesn't cost us anything, so not only are we generating clean energy, but the town is making money," he told Miguel.

In nearby Navarra, some local residents now invest in solar panels to generate funds for retirement.

North America is catching on—from Ontario to a number of U.S. states and cities. In Gainesville, Florida, a FIT ordinance passed with remarkable speed in 2009, and now residents who produce renewable energy no longer pay out 13 cents per kilowatt hour for electricity—instead, they *earn* 32 cents a kilowatt hour. And after relentless pushing from citizens, the U.K. is developing a FIT law for small renewables.

A barrier to renewables, laments Miguel, is the myth that they can provide only a small share of our energy.[249] Dead wrong, he says. Many studies and new practices are showing how—using new storage technologies, improved efficiency, and smart grid systems able to balance supply and demand—reliable, safe, and cost-effective renewable energy can provide up to 100 percent of our needs.[250]

Most importantly, Miguel reminds us, unlike in "old centralized, monopolized, energy systems, this smart, decentralized approach allows citizens and communities to learn and to invest. We all become part of the solution." So democratization of energy means "more innovation, problem solving, and entrepreneurialism."[251]

And if you still need motivation to act?

Note that polluting coal plants are being built at the pace of nearly two a week in China alone.[252]

### Entry point 3 Individually and together, citizens choose "power shopping."

Which head of lettuce you pick up today or where you buy your next T-shirt may not seem like a world-changing decision. But it is.

The *Spiral of Powerlessness* inside of the front cover is generated not only by laws on the books but by norms that our daily acts create. If we buy pesticide-sprayed food, we're saying to the food industry, "Yes, yes, give me more of that." If we buy organic instead, we are stimulating its production. (Why do you think McDonald's serves organic milk in Sweden but not here?) True, these marketplace "votes" are grossly lopsided—for the more money one has, the more votes one gets—but our purchases make ripples nonetheless.

I say this not to make us feel guilty but to help us realize our power.

Sixty percent of Americans say sustainability is one factor they weigh when making a purchase.[253] Partly in response, in just two decades, roughly thirty thousand companies have joined some sort of business organization setting standards for responsible behavior—it's now a $40 billion market.[254]

Why the change? Perhaps it's that we're learning to see what's always been invisible before. We can now readily calculate the environmental impact of our daily choices at, for example, myfootprint.org.

And other new online tools are popping up. Co-op America offers its National Green Pages guide to environmentally sound businesses online.[255]

The latest and most ambitious tool is GoodGuide at goodguide.com, still in its beta stage. It has created a smart shoppers' "app" for cell phones that can instantly offer information on the health, safety, and fairness-to-workers attributes of a product that catches my eye, right in the store. By simply scanning the item's barcode with an iPhone, or texting the name of the product to GoodGuide with a cell phone, one can gain access to over 50 thousand product ratings.[256]

The Fair Trade movement featured in Chapter 4 is a boon to "power shopping." Worldwide, its sales jumped by almost 50 percent in 2007, with consumers spending nearly $4.2 billion on fair-trade products by 2008.[257] Virtually unheard of here a decade ago, today over 70 percent of U.S. consumers recognize the Fair Trade term.[258] It now functions in almost sixty countries and has grown far beyond coffee.

Simply because consumers around the world are seeking out the Fair Trade label guaranteeing that producers receive a decent return, 7.5 million poor people are benefiting worldwide. Just a taste of its impact: In 2006, Rwandan coffee co-operatives, whose members include widows and orphans of the 1994 genocide, received a Fair Trade price for their coffee three times what local merchants offered.

This sea change in awakening to the power of our selective purchasing comes to us thanks to some energetic, determined people. One is Lina Musayev. Now in her late twenties, Lina was a student at

George Washington University when her life changed forever during a 2002 Oxfam America intensive leadership training course.

"Farmers from Guatemala came to talk to us," Lina told me. "We got the real story of Fair Trade from the roots. I didn't know anything about the coffee crisis. I didn't know it affected twenty-five million people. So when I heard about Fair Trade, I thought, 'This is incredible. It's working. It's making a difference.'

"The next day, literally, my friend Stephanie Faith Green, who'd come with me from Georgetown University, and I founded United Students for Fair Trade.

"She and I made a great team.

"Once school started, I decided to start with a petition saying students wanted more Fair Trade coffee. And we got two thousand students to sign—that's out of ten thousand. It worked. We sent a letter to Starbucks. We pushed for Fair Trade coffee at every university event."

I asked Lina what approach she'd found most effective in reaching students, and her response confirmed a theme of this book: As we replace anonymity with human connection, our natural empathy can kick in.

"The main thing is getting farmers themselves to come to the campus," Lina told me. "Hearing the farmers, I see the students say, 'Oh, my gosh—I didn't know this.' Almost like I was!"

After three years, George Washington University officially called upon all on-campus vending outlets to serve 100 percent Fair Trade coffee. In just five years, the student Fair Trade movement that Lina and her friend Stephanie launched has spread to one hundred fifty campuses, with many schools serving only Fair Trade.

Lina and Stephanie would probably find it hard ever again to view economics as simply about things exchanged in anonymous transactions. They've helped shape a new norm: an economy that's about people, people relating with each other—fairly.

Power shopping is an entry point—in part because of its empowering effect on the purchaser—as long as we keep foremost in mind that for the market to serve life we must operate not only as shoppers but also as citizens. There is no either/or here. We can be "power shoppers" and as citizens vote for those supporting rules that enable the market to serve life, including fair minimum wages and fair conditions for all workers—and that means farm workers, too—as well as standards that hold companies accountable. (Recall the horrific number of workplace-related deaths noted in Chapter 2?)

## COURSE CHANGER 2: *FROM A CULTURE OF VICTIMS AND BLAMERS TO A CULTURE OF EMPOWERMENT AND MUTUALITY*

Throughout, I've argued that there's plenty of evidence that almost all of us, not just a few "activists," want to be do-ers, actors in our world, not mere spectators. We want to be helpers. In fact, our well-being seems to depend on it. Human beings thrive when we feel useful; we wilt when we feel like burdens on others, or invisible with nothing to contribute. Living Democracy responds to this obvious aspect of human nature.

Among thousands and thousands of examples emerging—from community-supported agriculture and backyard gardening to children restoring the ravine near their school to community boards helping in the sentencing of, and restitutions made by, nonviolent offenders—here are two entry points that shift our culture:

### Entry point 1 Neighbors use new tools for mutual exchange, weaving communities together.

Twenty-five years ago, law school professor Edgar Cahn found himself in an intensive care unit recovering from a major heart attack, suddenly reliant on others. He felt useless and started to wonder about other so-called "throwaway people"—the elderly, the young, the sick, the poor.

He imagined that many felt like he did. They didn't want to be treated like helpless victims, and they hungered to contribute.

A lean and serious man, now in his early seventies, Edgar invented an elegantly simple tool, a tax-exempt "currency" not meant for buying more stuff but for getting help we might need—and, just as important, that we can "earn by helping others."

He calls it "Time Dollars," whereby one hour of service provided earns the provider an hour of service in return—be it walking a neighbor's dog, providing a lift to a doctor's appointment, raking leaves, stuffing envelopes, cooking meals, giving music lessons, running errands, or lending professional advice. You earn Time Dollars for each service you perform and then spend it on whatever you want from listings in an online Time Bank.

The key for Edgar is that every person's time has equal value. A babysitter's hour is worth no more or less than a lawyer's hour.

The Time Dollars approach helps to uproot all three dangerous conditions that rob us of our humanity—the conditions with which I began this book. It helps disperse power, because solutions are arising from regular citizens; they are creating new power—their own. It helps to strengthen community bonds, replacing anonymity; and it reinforces the principle of mutual accountability, the opposite of simple finger-pointing.

The Washington, D.C., Time Bank headquarters offers software participants use to easily keep track of "offers and requests," make contact with each other, and schedule gatherings. The approach has quickly spread to fifty centers in the United States and to thirteen other countries. For a nifty tour of the Time Dollars software that gives you a feeling for how it all works, visit timedollars.org.

Beyond Time Dollar exchanges, the invention of complementary paper currencies, useable only in a specific locality, are also "building connection with community of place," here and around the world, say leaders of the most successful U.S. example—Berkshares launched in western Massachusetts in 2006. Roughly $2.4 million worth of Berkshares are now circulating.

### Entry point 2 Young people, no longer dismissed as dependents and problems, become decision makers and contributors.

An "issue" is kids failing in school and getting into trouble with the law, especially poor kids. But probing more deeply to find an entry point, we realize that beneath that failure are feelings of powerlessness, hopelessness, and lack of self-valuing.

In Washington, D.C., Edgar Cahn used the Time Dollar approach when he founded Teen Courts, in which peers judge nonviolent youth offenders. An ex-offender then has a chance to contribute by serving on a jury, where he or she earns Time Dollars that can then be used to buy a recycled computer.

Among the one-quarter of youth offenders in Washington, D.C., who have been assigned to such courts, only 15 to 17 percent get into trouble again, a fraction of the typical re-offense rate.[259] Imagine the revolutionary potential of the youth court in a city where more than half of all young black men aged eighteen to twenty-four are under court jurisdiction.

Edgar's approach is alive in schools, too. Believing that the need to give is as deep for kids as for adults, he told Chicago school authorities to "find us any fifth and sixth graders willing to put in about a hundred hours tutoring younger kids and earn a recycled computer. The schools sent us the special education kids and those with attention-deficit problems," Edgar said.

As students went from being "underachievers" to becoming mentors, attendance went up on tutoring days, and fighting after school stopped—"because tutors didn't let anyone beat up their tutees," Edgar noted. Positive change happened as the children became givers, not just receivers—fulfilling a deep human need.

And then there's YouthBuild, also building power and connection.

In 1978, a former Harlem elementary school teacher in her thirties, Dorothy Stoneman, wanted to do her part to uproot the racism and poverty hurting her students. Realizing the power of young people themselves, she asked East Harlem teenagers a straightforward question: "What would you do to improve your community if you had adult support?"

"We'd rebuild the houses. We'd take empty buildings back from the drug dealers and eliminate crime," they told her. Together, they and Dorothy formed what became YouthBuild to renovate a tenement building.

Since then, ninety-two thousand young people, living in poor communities and previously unable to see a future, have through YouthBuild produced over nineteen thousand units of affordable housing. Many have at the same time earned their GED, apprenticed in the building trades, and learned the arts of democracy.

YouthBuilders experience themselves not as recipients of help but as powerful contributors, says Dorothy (who, I am happy to say, is now my friend). Besides their construction achievements and academic gains, they also help raise funds and share in leading the national organization.

The young people even help choose staff. In fact, Dorothy once told me that the only hiring mistake at YouthBuild happened when once she overrode the judgment of the youth. "They told me he [Dorothy's pick] didn't show enough real understanding, but I thought I needed his other skills. I was wrong," said Dorothy.

The movement has spread to two hundred seventy-three sites reaching almost all states. Its success has earned federal funds, now via the Department of Labor; and YouthBuild is being called to other countries, starting with South Africa and Mexico, Central America, Israel, and Canada.

"Without YouthBuild, I would probably be dead or in jail," graduates have told Dorothy. "Instead I am building homes, going to college, and making a difference." And, she reminds me, "YouthBuild graduates don't just have tools helping *them* live better. They've become citizens and leaders making the world better for us all."

### Entry point 3 Citizens move from spectators to public problem solvers.

In recent decades, invisible to most of us, citizens are playing increasingly critical roles in shaping solutions to public problems. They are living proof of something increasingly recognized by social scientists—that better ideas arise in encounters with diverse perspectives. Just a taste of what I mean:

**Study circles.** Typically, they involve eight to twelve people who come together with the help of a trained facilitator, explore an issue, and come up with action steps. Nearly two million Swedes participate each year in almost 300,000 study circles.[260] The chief promoter of U.S. study circles is East Hartford-based Everyday Democracy. (Remember the impact of study circles in Kansas City and the leader of Everyday Democracy, Martha McCoy, who opened Chapter 4?)

Since 1989, Everyday Democracy has worked with more than six hundred U.S. communities, tackling everything from community racial divides to school reforms. In the late '90s, for example, 1,300 citizens came together in eighty-two single-session study circles, organized by Sedgwick County, Kansas, to weigh waste disposal options. When the circles picked recycling as their first priority, the county enlisted corporate help and launched county-wide recycling. Several months later, eight hundred residents convened in study circles again to work through specifics, which the county then incorporated into its waste plan.[261]

**21st Century Town Hall Meeting.** Developed by Washington-based AmericaSpeaks, the 21st Century Town Hall Meeting is a briefer, technology-assisted approach to tapping citizen wisdom. Founder Carolyn Lukensmeyer has an amazing gift for bringing people together to produce results. She wants you to be clear, though: This is not a "public hearing"—no Q & A, no panels.

Rather, a large body—five hundred to five thousand people—are divided into diverse groups of ten to twelve who engage in round-table discussions, assisted by a trained facilitator. Written guides provide background. Each facilitator uses a laptop networked to other laptops in the room, so each table's ideas and conclusions can be quickly transmitted to a theme team. That team synthesizes all of it and on a large screen presents the synthesis to everybody. Participants then use individual keypads to vote on the synthesized recommendations.

In 1993, for example, AmericaSpeaks organized such a 21st Century Town Hall Meeting called Americans Discuss Social Security. Since then, they've continued to work on some of our country's most critical challenges, ranging from the redevelopment of lower Manhattan after September 11th to the revival of New Orleans following 2005's Hurricane Katrina.[262]

Imagine what a cacophony of accusation and misinformation we would have been spared had the Obama administration used the approach in early 2009 to help Americans grapple with health insurance reform. Think of it: Tens of thousands of Americans, armed with essential, balanced background materials and facilitators, meeting face-to-face in libraries and social halls, debating options, weighing pros and cons, and then registering our ideas in a national online, transparent database to guide Congress and the president.

Other fascinating formats for effective citizen deliberation include the Deliberative Dialogue, Citizens Jury, and Citizen Assembly, all used in the United States and around the world. To learn more about these emerging Living Democracy practices that link face-to-face talk with big public problems, visit the Coalition for Dialogue and Deliberation at thataway.org.

## COURSE CHANGER 3: *FROM POLITICS DRIVEN BY MONEY TO POLITICS DRIVEN BY CITIZENS' VALUES*

This course changer comes last because it is first—the Mother of All Issues.

Whether we're working to empower young people and re-knit our communities, remaking the market's logic via laws that reward renewable energy producers, or setting new rules that hold companies accountable for the entire lifecycle of their products, none of our efforts can reach the scale of impact required as long as "privately held government" still rules.

We can take heart, though: There's now a pathway of escape from a politics of plutonomy (to use Citigroup's useful descriptor)—a pathway charted by courageous citizens.

### Entry point 1 Citizens persuade lawmakers to enact "voluntary public financing" of elections and to block corporate influence.

When it comes to our broken politics, here, too, one can always settle for an "issue"—electing a principled candidate, for example. But that alone won't do the job. Since a major cause of thinning democracy is the power of money over political decision making, the entry point is *removing that power*. And the best kept secret in America is that it is both possible *and* already happening in the legislatures of three states—Maine came first; then Arizona and Connecticut. Several more states use Clean Elections for a number of important offices.[263]

So citizens are reducing the power of private interests within government, while significantly increasing citizens' voices and trust in government and each other. Recall, for example, Maine's groundbreaking producer-responsibility law, described a few pages back. It changed the logic of the market as producers were made accountable for the lifecycle of their products.

And *how* did it get by the electronic industry's lobbyists?

"It was an uphill battle," Maine environmental leader Pete Didisheim said. Industry lobbyists mounted the biggest effort ever in this state. But because of the Clean Elections law, they couldn't "sprinkle campaign checks across the State House to help kill the bill. All the big computer makers—IBM, Panasonic, Mitsubishi... did put tens of millions into TV and print ads opposing it. Apple, despite its progressive image, was the worst. Only Hewlett-Packard supported the bill. It sees recovery of used computers as a business opportunity."

But how is it possible to achieve Clean Elections, given the lock-down of money on the system? Well, let me introduce you to Marge Mead of Sun City, Arizona. Marge, mother of eight, grandmother of ten, took her first college class when she was forty-two and got her master's degree at fifty-one. But, after years of teaching, "I was tired of correcting freshman compositions," she told me, "so I retired, and my husband and I moved here to Sun City."

She felt like a fish out of water until she attended a meeting of the local Democratic Club. Soon Marge became a precinct and state committee person. She joined the League of Women Voters.

In 1996, several League leaders were going to be away for the summer, and Marge was asked to fill in at meetings to shape a law to clean up campaigns. "I was pretty ignorant about details of the law," Marge said, "and ignorant about politics in general."

But she felt strongly about money's corrupting power. "Big campaign donors aren't in it for altruism," she said. "They don't consider their money a contribution; they consider it an investment." (And a pretty sound one, too.)

So Marge went to the campaign finance reform meeting as a stand-in. The goal was "Clean Elections" in Arizona. The means: a voluntary system of public finance in which candidates hoping to receive public funds must collect a certain number of small "qualifying contributions" from registered voters. Then the candidate takes no private money, and the government provides a fixed sum for campaigning. If clean elections candidates are outspent by privately funded opponents, they may receive additional public matching funds.

"I walked in and said, 'Who's taking notes?'

Marge's insistence on taking the minutes herself launched what she called her "latest incarnation, that of political activist"—a citizen leader in a critical battle for democracy.

"I was in awe," she told me. "It was a new concept and rather radical. I was amazed at the dedication of other members of the coalition.

"At first, I felt insecure; the law is complicated. But I traveled all over the place talking to various groups. I went to Glendale Community College, where I had been an instructor, and talked to social studies classes. It was exhilarating, and I became increasingly confident."

To bring the Clean Elections Act to a vote, the coalition had to collect 10 percent of the number of votes cast for governor in the previous election—that was 112,961 signatures. "And when it came to the vote, we [voluntary public financing] squeaked by with 51 percent," Marge said.

The law took effect in 1998. In no time, wealthy narrow-interest groups, accustomed to buying the attention of politicians, began battling Clean Elections. Bankers, developers, and corporate lobbyists—calling themselves No Taxpayer Money for

Politicians—spent half a million dollars trying to put a dubiously worded question on the 2004 ballot to kill Clean Elections in Arizona.

They failed. And by 2008—just ten years after Marge and the League's success—two-thirds of the Arizona legislature had gained their seats using "clean elections" funding.[264]

Clean Elections didn't start in Arizona with grandma Marge and her League buddies, though. Maine can claim that honor: It came first in 1996, when twenty-six-year-old political science grad David Donnelly helped launch the reform. Today over 80 percent of Maine's legislators have "run clean."

Not only is the Clean Elections Act a major reason Maine has been able to lead the nation in environmental protection, for example; it has opened the door to new talent, too. Without Clean Elections "I wouldn't have dared to try," says Mainer Deb Simpson. Now in her forties, Deb was a waitress and single mom in 2000, but friends spotted leadership in her and encouraged her to run for office. Elected to Maine's house that year, then re-elected, she now serves in the state senate, where she sits on the Natural Resources Committee.

Deb's story so powerfully illustrates what can happen when money is not the driver that we've created a web documentary of her story, viewed from smallplanet.org.[265]

Armed with proof that voluntary public financing, "Clean Elections," draws candidates and voters in, and keeps money out, citizens in dozens of states are busy crafting similar laws.[266]

And at the federal level?

In early 2010 a Fair Elections Now Act is pending in both houses of Congress, with prominent bipartisan support. To be eligible for public support, a congressional candidate first has to meet a threshold of small donations. Then he or she can accept contributions only up to $100; these are then matched four to one by a public campaign fund—for a total large enough to support a viablecampaign; the candidate also enjoys reduced fees for TV airtime. A similar bill covering the presidential race is being drafted.

In November 2008, 69 percent of Americans polled supported the approach. Now is the moment to get Fair Elections passed: Many Americans are outraged at the power of corporate lobbyists, and President Obama says he'll support the law. You'll find all you need to act at change-congress.org, Youstreet.org, commoncause.org, or publicampaign.org.

As noted , in 2010 the Supreme Court ruled corporate political-spending restrictions unconstitutional. The ruling doesn't derail the Clean Elections (Fair Elections) approach because in it the candidate's choice to rely on public funds is voluntary; but it does make enactment more urgent. The Court's conflation of spending and speech, and real humans and corporations, is an affront to democracy with huge implications. It could limit our right to choose among diverse candidates—those beyond the tiny slice of us favored by corporations—and much more.

Despair, however, isn't an option. So diverse groups are devising strategies to blunt and reverse the ruling's impact. Long-term approaches involve the make-up of the Court itself and passing a constitutional amendment. But with millions outraged by the

Court's anti-democratic ruling, let's push back for democracy, now. One possibility? Legislation requiring that a corporation have shareholder approval before spending to influence an election and be prominently named in any political advertising it sponsors. Never has it been more important for citizens to join in dialogue and action for the heart and soul of democracy.

### Entry point 2 Making election rules fairer, citizens can be heard and trust that they are.

As Clean Elections jump to the top of our can-do list, we can also support several other relatively easy reforms that make a huge difference for the emergence of Living Democracy.

One is "*instant run-off*" voting, used in a number of citywide races across the country, including San Francisco, Burlington, Vermont, and Minneapolis.[268] It means that as a voter I get to rank candidates by my preference rather than having to choose only one. Then, if no one candidate receives a majority of the votes, the candidate with the fewest votes gets out, and the votes are counted. If my top-ranked candidate fails to make it to this next round, my vote transfers automatically to my second choice. That way, I never have to fear "wasting" my precious vote by supporting a dark horse. Instant run-off voting gives all of us a way to know the real range of an electorate's views, and encourages people to vote even if they fear their favorite will lose.[269]

Second, what could be more unfair than our Electoral College system? If a presidential candidate wins states with a lot of electoral votes, he or she can be elected even while losing the popular vote. It has happened four times. The Electoral College is thus an insult to citizens, an anti-democratic anachronism reflecting distrust of the public. In addition to the unlikely but possible outcome of the citizens' choice being overridden, the system means some citizens get much less attention from candidates: The Electoral College gives presidential candidates little reason to poll, visit, advertise, or organize in states that are clear wins or clear losses for them.

So support is growing to *make the national popular vote the decider* in presidential elections.

The change does not require a constitutional amendment if state legislatures pass laws instructing the Electoral College to pick as the winner the biggest popular vote getter. With that simple step, the Electoral College's power over us is history. To trigger the change, all that's needed is for states whose Electoral College votes total enough to elect a president (270 of 538) to pass such a law. Already states with about a quarter of the needed votes have done so; and almost two thousand state legislators are on record in favor of the step. It takes little time for each of us to urge this key democratic reform at nationalpopularvote.com.

Finally, let's never forget Thomas Paine's insight: Voting "is the right upon which all other rights depend." Yet in Ohio alone, in the 2004 presidential election, that right was violated for at least 357,000 voters, mostly Democratic. They were blocked from casting ballots or their votes weren't counted.[270] We can support efforts to prevent the repetition of this travesty, for "if people lose faith that their votes are accurately and faithfully recorded," Robert Kennedy, Jr., warns, "they will abandon the ballot box."[271]

Wherever we are, we can talk up and support these doable, straightforward, and revolutionary course changes and the entry points they suggest.

## BREAKING THE SPELL

Too often, way too often, as I speak publicly, I sense an audience is with me till I get to the final points above—until I really begin to explain how we can reclaim politics and that it is doable.

Too many eyes glaze over.

Media pundits of both the Left and the Right have also been audibly silent: In 2009 journalists and scholars offered plenty of vivid exposés of Big Finance and Big Health Insurance lobbyists blocking real reform. But rarely, very rarely, did thought leaders go beyond outrage to the only real solution: reform that would remove these lobbyists' power and let democracy work.

Only we can break this spell. May the shock of the Supreme Court's 2010 ruling, unleashing limitless corporate political spending, shatter the silence.

We can't have the world we want if we can't choose leaders who answer to us. It may seem huge, but at least it is that simple. So together we can find the terms, the metaphors, the stories—like that of Deb Simpson, who went from waitress to influential state senator—to stop eyes from glazing over. We can make this Number One question of democracy come to life for us and our friends.

## AN INTERNAL CHECKLIST

Joyful living, I'm convinced, happens when we hit that spot where a potent entry point that touches root causes also fires our own deep passions. I know that, once I discovered that spot—by asking, "Why hunger amidst plenty?" in my twenties—it set off a personal revolution, and I've been forever grateful.

To find that spot, a critical first step may be to recognize that the negative spiral can start deep inside us. If a feeling of "lack" lurks at the center of our pain, pain that we then project out and create in the world, we can start within ourselves to reverse it. Right now, we can focus on the strengths in ourselves and our loved ones and the possibilities right in front of our noses.

Think of something you are doing right now that makes you feel strong. Maybe you are engaged in your children's schools to make them more empowering for students; or helping to shift our society's failing frame by posting your opinions on a blog or your Facebook page; or sending off an email to the newspaper shaping your community's views. (Remember that even if it's not printed, someone has read it and registered a reader's concerns.)

Maybe you just became a supporter of your community radio station, or you are exploring whether your congregation might join the three million Americans working for basic fairness in our society through their faith communities. Maybe you've chosen to convert your home to solar energy, or to join in "community-supported agriculture" by buying a share in a nearby farm's produce. Or you are finally speaking out about discrimination you see at work.

Then think about what you've always wanted to do as you mull over the three "course changers" here, asking how your own passions align or don't align with the frame I'm proposing.

In figuring out how best to use my own capacities, it helps me to keep asking, *"How do I know Living Democracy when I see it?"*

So I've developed *Idea 8*, Living Democracy's Checklist, organized around five big questions. I hope it can help you weigh whether a given approach is interrupting the destructive causal flow and speeding the life-enhancing *Spiral of Empowerment.*

## Idea 8: Living Democracy's Checklist

as we probe deeply, identify causal patterns, & choose entry points

### AM I EXPANDING AND SPREADING POWER?

- ☐ Does my action create new power, greater awareness, and strengthening of my own and others' capacities? Does it reduce power imbalances?
- ☐ Is my effort contributing to a one-time correction, or does it generate ongoing, fairer and more effective decision making?
- ☐ Does accountability flow one-way, or are multiple parties taking responsibility and being held accountable?

### AM I EASING FEAR OF CHANGE AND FEAR OF THE OTHER?

- ☐ Am I modeling that it's okay to be afraid as we face the new?
- ☐ Does my effort replace stereotyping with valuing and welcoming diversity?
- ☐ Am I helping to build group bonds that strengthen courage without excluding others?

### AM I LEARNING AND TEACHING THE ARTS OF DEMOCRACY?

- ☐ Does my effort teach and practice active listening, the creative use of conflict, ongoing evaluation, mentoring, and other essential skills for effectiveness?

### AM I CREATING MOVEMENT THAT IS SUSTAINABLE?

- ☐ Is the initiative made inherently rewarding with big doses of real learning, humor, beauty, celebration, and camaraderie?
- ☐ Is it being made widely visible so that those beyond the inner circle are motivated to act? (Don't forget our mirror neurons!)

### AM I REPLACING THE LIMITING FRAME WITH AN EMPOWERING ONE?

- ☐ Am I helping to replace the core presumption of "lack" with that of "possibility"?
- ☐ Am I helping to replace belief in fixed economic laws with confidence in human creativity?
- ☐ Am I refocusing us on the goodness "in" human nature—our needs for connection, fairness, and effectiveness—we can tap to heal our beautiful planet?

## JUSTICE, PLEASE MEET DEMOCRACY

I began this chapter suggesting that in order to unleash our own energy we need to see causal pattern. Without that, our acts can feel like "random acts of sanity." Satisfying at first, they ultimately feel futile if we can't see how they interrupt underlying forces spreading pain and move us in a positive direction.

I've also argued that the aphorism "seeing is believing" is sweet but wrong. The way human brains are made, *believing is seeing*. And the only way to believe in the new is to become part of it. As my daughter Anna Lappé and I traveled the world to write *Hope's Edge*, we observed that the most hopeful people, those with the greatest sense of possibility, were hardly the most advantaged. What they did have in common was easy to spot: They were taking the biggest risks. They were engaged, heart and soul.

> *Hope is not what we find in evidence. It is what we become in action.*
>
> —MOTTO OF THE SMALL PLANET INSTITUTE

And to jump in, most of us need to feel that we are part of something larger. So what I'm aiming for is not simply raising awareness about the root of our global crisis or multiplying disparate positive acts.

This is happening.

At a holiday party this year, attended mostly by people I didn't know, two of the three guests with whom I shared the most talk time, an elder and a young mother, glowed as one described her large community garden in the service of a soup kitchen, and the other excitedly described staying up till 2 a.m. finishing a business plan to become a full-time farmer. They, and many others, are searching for meaning, and finding it in such work.

I want that, and I want more. And I bet they do, too. I want to feel part of a connected, growing global movement. My yearning may be felt by millions, maybe even billions.

A *movement*?

Yes. An everyday feeling that I'm walking shoulder-to-shoulder with people around the world, eagerly exploring root causes and consciously evolving language and ways of seeing that capture more and more imaginations because they have explanatory power. Such a movement is not just about multiplying sane acts. It has coherence, a shape. It evolves in dialogue across cultures and continents, drawing us into a community of shared meaning—not a new dogma, but a purposeful, satisfying common exploration.

It grows not from wishful thinking but from what we humans are learning about ourselves. In it, we each can know we're offering up our own special piece of a whole cloth.

It is a Living Democracy movement, and I want to be part of it.

## JUSTICE AND DEMOCRACY—SOFT-WIRED PARTNERS

My sentiment isn't sixties' nostalgia, I promise. The sixties proved for my generation, and those following, what organized, gutsy citizens can do—from advancing civil rights to helping end a war. But I have no illusions. While the sixties generation valued and fought for honesty, justice and participation, we lacked a coherent vision.

Notwithstanding the era's iconic communes and "flower children," the sixties largely continued the work of a long and glorious line of courageous fighters for justice. This sense of justice—motivating us to make explicit rules and to punish violators—seems to be soft-wired in us, allowing us to recognize the potential bully out there, as well as the one inside. While foundational to our humanity, our sense of justice is, mostly, reactive—countering threats, resisting oppression, overthrowing tyrants.

In 2010, Supreme Court Justice John Roberts' sense of justice apparently made him angry that any entity, not just a person but a non-human corporation—one, say, as big as Royal Dutch Shell whose wealth would rank it as the world's twenty-fifth largest economy—might have limits imposed on its influence in selecting political leaders. His passion, helping create a 5-4 decision allowing unlimited corporate political spending, derives from seeing justice as the right to do as one chooses unless directly harming another.

But this narrow frame can blind us to ruinous harm.

It not only defeats itself if it speeds or excuses the concentration of power we now know generates vast injustice, but it also subordinates our duty to ourselves and others to respond to positive human needs that only democracy can satisfy. They include the need of each of us real human beings, not just the Royal Dutch Shells, to have a voice in our future, and the need to live in thriving communities where everyone has the opportunity to participate.

These two, justice and democracy, live or die together. Just as the need for justice is soft-wired in us, so, I've argued throughout, is our capacity for empathy and our need for agency and cooperation—exactly what democracy protects and nurtures. We Americans face, therefore, a defining moment. This Court's ruling, if not reversed or its impact deflected through legislation, could help to kill democracy and, with it, justice.

Curiously, we have far better grasped the need to defend rights and to punish the "badness" in us, even if we have a hard time doing it, than we have the need to cultivate the "goodness," including our yearning to have a voice in thriving communities. Now is the moment for both. We can join our passion for justice with our joy in learning to live democracy—creating the rules and daily norms and practices promoting the best in us. With both, it becomes possible to correct our course as we head toward calamity.

## BOLD HUMILITY

But how do we ignite a movement—*become* a movement?

First, remember that we don't need confidence in success, as João Pedro Stédile reminded me. We need only to believe in possibility. And, making it easier, I'm discovering a new kind of humility: When I add up just about everything that most inspires me in the world, I have to admit that I would have given these efforts almost zero probability of success when I was my children's age.

Unschooled village women in Kenya defying authorities and planting forty-five million trees? No way. But they did it. Poor landless people in Brazil creating thousands of new villages, schools, and businesses in the most effective land reform in the western world? Not a chance. But they did it. A ragtag handful of Wisconsin farmers banding together, as their neighbors' farms folded, to build a multi-million dollar, democratic business? Nah, not possible. But they did it.

All that's humbling.

Real humility, I now see, is admitting that *it is not possible to know what's possible*. And if this is true, we are free. We are free to go for the world we really want, unhindered by the false idea that we should calculate our action based on probabilities of success.

After all, most of the Living Democracy initiatives you've encountered in this book began with one person or a small handful of people. The rapidity of their growth, the parallels in the lessons being learned, suggests that we would be naïve—just plain silly—to underestimate their potential to scale, enabling us to truly live democracy.

## CIVIL COURAGE

With these insights, we can then get serious about *why* so many of us tolerate the intolerable.

In the first chapter I offer a theory. My theory is that we humans are plenty "good enough," but somewhere along the way most of us lost our capacity to stand up for ourselves. As I argue in Chapter 9, we're soft-wired to fear embarrassment—or worse—if we break from the pack. So we shut up. We go along.

And, as I argue in Chapter 1, the very complexity of our magnificent brains makes us vulnerable to the power of ideas—including those "big ideas" shaping an entire social order, those mental maps powerful enough either to stunt us or to free us.

*So if we're good enough, what do we need more of?*

What Professor Otto Herz in Leipzig taught me to call "civil courage." It means being willing to say the unpopular and to say what has to be said, even when it upsets another or makes their eyes glaze over! It means not being defeated when we encounter upset or disinterest, but becoming even more determined.

If courage is the critical missing ingredient in turning our planet toward life, how do we get more of it?

The new neuroscience gives us a big clue. Observing others actually changes us, we now know, because of our "mirror neurons." Remember them in Chapter 5? Those neurons in our brains that fire when we are observing something: They mimic the activity in our brain that occurs when we ourselves perform the action. So, as we observe those more courageous than we, we take into ourselves a bit of their courage.

In order to multiply the courageous, we can actively protect, publicly reward, and honor truth tellers—including those risking humiliation, livelihoods, or their lives to uphold democratic values.

Ever hear of Brooksley Born? She is the former chair of the Commodity Futures Trade Commission who stood virtually alone in warning that an unregulated derivatives market would lead to ruin, even when other powerful voices, including Alan Greenspan and key legislators, basically told her to get lost.[272]

Or Marcy Kaptur? She is the Ohio representative who encouraged her constituents facing foreclosure to resist eviction orders because of what she saw as the irresponsibility of lenders.[273]

Or Russ Feingold? He is the Wisconsin senator who stood alone in 2001 against the Patriot Act and was one of only twenty-three senators to vote against the Iraq war.[274]

Or the eighty-eight professors at Tehran University? In early 2010 they signed a letter to Iran's supreme leader asking him to end violence against protesters, knowing full well the risks they were taking.[275]

Or the brave Afghan schoolgirls? In 2009 they banded together and continued their education even after a violent attack by men opposed to educating females had disfigured a classmate on her way to school.

We can intentionally seek out courage. That's the lesson of this new neuroscience. We can choose our heroes well, and study them. We can our choose buddies well. We can pick those embodying the qualities we want to fortify in ourselves.

Finding even one can make the difference. Psychologist Solomon Asch's experiments—where subjects deny what their own eyes tell them—show that often all it takes is a single ally to enable us to stay true to ourselves. Knowing this, we can seek out those who encourage us to risk for what we believe in.

To build courage making it possible to live democracy, we can reward our children from the earliest ages for speaking out against unfairness and for taking responsibility for setting and enforcing rules, as is part of the school mediation training highlighted in Chapter 6.

Recently, an acquaintance told me that Lech Walesa, when asked how Solidarity, the Polish freedom movement, got started, answered: "We began by talking loudly at bus stops." It may be apocryphal, but it works for me.

So we can bulk up our civil-courage muscle by simply breaking the silence and talking about what matters most in the world—at office parties, around the kitchen table, during our congregation's social hour, at the diner or coffee shop.

We can challenge pundits and reform advocates, too, who repeat the refrain that our problem is poverty, global warming, or hunger, and fail to identify these issues as mere *symptoms* of the deeper problem—the lack of real, Living Democracy. We can challenge leaders to anchor their particular missions in this deeper frame.

In this vein, please recall my own "test" of strength, which I only partially passed in my encounter with Congressman Gerlach in Chapter 7. I hope my story helps you prepare yourself to do better than I.

We can find such strength inside us as we come to see that indeed there is no physical barrier in our path. The barrier is inside. Not in our evil nature, but only in our gullibility, in unthinkingly falling for ideas—about who we are and the impossibility of real democracy—that are unworthy of us.

## OUR MOMENT

So now is our moment, our species' do-or-die moment. The good news is that we are free to act on the truth about ourselves, and it may not be too late to change course.

For the first time humans have the perspective of our long evolutionary journey—from fair sharers to too many frantic shoppers, from a lot of cooperators to too many dominators—all in the same gene lines. We have the perspective of eerie lab experiments in which we have been the guinea pigs and don't come out looking so good. We have the perspective of neuroscientists, cognitive scientists, evolutionary anthropologists, and more, among whom there appears to be growing consensus about our deep, pro-social needs and capacities.

Whew. We can breathe. There is enough goodness in us and in nature that we don't have to run away from ourselves; we don't have to invent myths to escape or distort reality. We can follow our endless curiosity about the real nature of life and living, and we'll be okay. We can thrive.

We can trust our deep, inborn needs to connect and affect. We can trust our ability to walk with fear. We can even trust our capacity to let go of long-held ways of seeing in order to structure our societies to protect us from the worst in us while releasing the best—for we know in our bones that real problems facing our planet can only be met by the ingenuity, experience, and buy-in—the contagious engagement—of billions of us.

Knowing all this, it is at least possible that we can take the biggest leap, embracing the open and dynamic frame that Living Democracy offers us. And in this crucial evolutionary step, we can celebrate the truth that neither justice nor democracy can achieve their potential without being hand-in-hand with, in love with, each other.

With this union, reflecting two essential dimensions of our humanity, I believe we can create ways of living worthy of our planet's needs and the best in us. In it, democracy in its current thin and failing form is giving way to democracy as a rewarding way of living—one that gets us up in the morning not just girded to denounce the latest outrage, but eager to co-create thriving communities—with good work, fortifying friendships, just rules, invigorating diversity, productive conflict, everyday beauty…and endless curiosity.

> *Life is so full of meaning and purpose, so full of beauty beneath its covering...*
> *Courage then to claim it; that is all!*
> *But courage you have, and the knowledge that we are pilgrims together,*
> *wending through unknown country home.*
>
> —FRA GIOCONDO GIOVANNI, LETTER, CHRISTMAS EVE 1513

# AN INVITATION

Thank you for engaging with the ideas in this book—ideas I hope will continue to evolve. I will make corrections with each printing, and later I will publish *Getting a Grip3* to incorporate new learning: So please send me your ideas via the Getting a Grip page at smallplanet.org.

Now, to my big question: Where do we go from here? In the final pages, I declared my own desire to be part of a Living Democracy movement. It felt like a big step. But what does the word "movement" *mean* in this context?

I am trying to understand. Are you curious, too?

Could there be a movement that is not made up of certain people, but rather of ideas—ideas that millions of people are sharing responsibility for infusing here, there, and everywhere? And are evolving in face-to-face dialogue?

People the world over are in fact "living democracy," I've argued in these pages. They are showing us all how. Yet, in early 2010 we're faced with a Supreme Court decision, unleashing corporate influence in politics, that defies the world's need, now more than ever, for empowered, engaged citizens.

Could this shock help to energize a Living Democracy movement, stimulating a process of conscious learning that shapes more and more settings—from our child's classroom to the way we engage in deliberating the strategies for removing the power of money from politics?

If you, too, are curious about where we go from here, please visit smallplanet.org and take a Living Democracy Quick Poll. See how your responses to these ideas relate to others'. Then offer your suggestions about how most effectively to further the emergence of Living Democracy and peruse other readers' suggestions. Weigh in on what a movement might mean to you; or whether that frame itself is a good idea. We're also eager for views on what Small Planet might best contribute and what you are most eager to do.

Think about creating a "living democracy" exploration group with friends (Meetup.com, founded by a friend of mine, could make it easy). Consider using the *Getting a Grip* group or class discussion guide at smallplanet.org to develop these ideas further and move them powerfully into the world.

I hope our curiosity will bring us all greater clarity, creativity, and courage.

Frances Moore Lappé
www.smallplanet.org

# RECOMMENDED READING

## BY THE PRINCIPALS OF THE SMALL PLANET INSTITUTE

Diet for a Hot Planet: The Climate Crisis at the End of Your Fork and What You Can Do About it
Anna Lappé

Liberation Ecology: Reframing Six Disempowering Ideas that Keep Us from Aligning With Nature—Even Our Own
Frances Moore Lappé

Democracy's Edge: Choosing to Save Our Country by Bringing Democracy to Life
Frances Moore Lappé

Diet for a Small Planet
Frances Moore Lappé

Grub: Ideas for an Urban Organic Kitchen Anna Lappé and Bryant Terry
Hope's Edge: The Next Diet for a Small Planet
Frances Moore Lappé and Anna Lappé

World Hunger: Twelve Myths
Frances Moore Lappé, Joseph Collins and Peter Rossett

You Have the Power: Choosing Courage in a Culture of Fear
Frances Moore Lappé and Jeffrey Perkins

## AND FROM OTHERS

The Anatomy of Human Destructiveness
Erich Fromm

Earth Democracy
Vandana Shiva

The Great Turning: From Empire to Earth Community
David Korten

Mindfulness
Ellen Langer

Mothers and Others: The Evolutionary Origins of Mutual Understanding
Sarah Blaffer Hrdy

The Next Form of Democracy
Matt Leighninger

Natural Capitalism
Paul Hawken, Amory and Hunter Lovins

Strong Democracy
Benjamin Barber

## PERIODICALS THAT OFTEN OFFER STORIES OF LIVING DEMOCRACY

Adbusters Magazine–Canada
E-mail: info@adbusters.org www.adbusters.org

Ode Magazine–The Netherlands
E-mail: ode@odemagazine.com www.odemagazine.com

New Internationalist–United Kingdom
www.newint.org

Resurgence Magazine–United Kingdom
www.resurgence.org

Utne Magazine–USA
www.utne.com

WorldWatch Magazine–USA
www.worldwatch.org/pubs/mag/

Yes! Magazine–USA
www.yesmagazine.org

## WEBSITES

Environmental News and Commentary
www.grist.org

Environmental Working Group
www.ewg.org

Institute for Agriculture and Trade Policy
www.iatp.org

Union of Concerned Scientists
www.ucsusa.org

Wiser Earth
www.wiserearth.org

World Changing, Change Your Thinking
www.worldchanging.org

World Future Council
www.worldfuturecouncil.org

# ENDNOTES

1 Food and Agriculture Organization of the United Nations, "Hunger Statistics-World," http://www.fao.org/hunger/en/ (accessed December 18, 2009); Robert B. Semple, Jr., "Hunger and Politics," *New York Times*, March 23, 1969; Food and Agriculture Organization of the United Nations, "The State of Food Insecurity in the World 2001," Economic and Social Development Department, 2001, http://www.fao.org/docrep/003/y1500e/y1500e03.htm.
2 Food and Agriculture Organization of the United Nations, "The State of Food Insecurity in the World—Economic Crisis: Impacts and Lessons Learned," Economic and Social Development Department, 2009, http://www.fao.org/publications/sofi/en/.
3 Food and Agriculture Organization of the United Nations, "Food and Agriculture Statistics Global Outlook," Statistics Division, June 2006, http://faostat.fao.org/Portals/_Faostat/documents/pdf/world.pdf.
4 Food and Agriculture Organization of the United Nations, "Hunger Statistics-World," http://www.fao.org/hunger/en/ (accessed December 7, 2009).
5 "Hunger in the United States," *New York Times*, November 17, 2009, http://www.nytimes.com/2009/11/18/opinion/18wed2.html?_r=1&scp=1&sq=editorial%20food%20insecure%20households&st=cse.
6 United Nations International Children's Emergency Fund, "UNICEF's Work," http://www.unicefusa.org/work/ (accessed on December 22, 2009).
7 "Suicide Prevention," World Health Organization, http://www.who.int/mental_health/prevention/suicide/suicideprevent/en/; See also: "Depression," http://www.who.int/mental_health/management/depression/definition/en/.
8 Nomi Prins, *It Takes a Pillage* (Hoboken, NJ: John Wiley & Sons, Inc., 2009), 216.
9 Gretchen Morgenson and Louise Story, "Banks Bundled Bad Debt, Bet Against It and Won," *New York Times*, December 24, 2009, http://www.nytimes.com/2009/12/24/business/24trading.html?_r=1&ref=todayspaper&pagewanted=print; Greg Gordon, "How Goldman Secretly Bet on the U.S. Housing Crash," McClatchy News, November 1, 2009, http://www.mcclatchydc.com/100/story/77791.html?storylink=omni_popular.
10 John Arlidge, "I'm Doing 'God's Work': Meet Mr. Goldman Sachs," TimesOnline, November 8, 2009, http://www.timesonline.co.uk/tol/news/world/us_and_americas/article6907681.ece
11 Charles Babington, "Bush: U.S. Must 'Rid the World of Evil'," *Washington Post*, September 14, 2001, http://www.washingtonpost.com/ac2/wp-dyn?pagename=article&node=&contentId=A30485-2001Sep14.
12 For information on prison statistics for 1987-2007, see: Pew Center on the States' Public Performance Safety Project, *One in 100: Behind Bars in America 2008* (Washington, DC: Pew Center on the States, 2008), 5, http://www.pewcenteronthestates.org/uploadedFiles/One%20in%20100.pdf; For information on prison statistics for 2008, see: U.S. Bureau of Justice Statistics, "Prisoners in 2008," December 8, 2008, http://bjs.ojp.usdoj.gov/index.cfm?ty=pbdetail&iid=1763; For information on executions, see: N.C. Aizenman, "New High in U.S. Prison Numbers," *Washington Post*, February 29, 2008, http://www.washingtonpost.com/wp-dyn/content/story/2008/02/28/ST2008022803016.html; *The Death Penalty in 2008: Year End Report* (Washington, DC: Death Penalty Information Center, December 2008), 1.
13 Sheldon Rampton and John Stauber, *Banana Republicans: How the Right Wing Is Turning America into a One-Party State* (New York: Tarcher/Penguin, 2004), 2.
14 Nicholas Wade, "We May be Born with an Urge to Help," *New York Times*, December 1, 2009.
15 Alexis de Tocqueville, *Democracy in America*, Book I, ch. 14, http://xroads.virginia.edu/~hyper/detoc/1_ch14.htm.

16 Bill McKibben, *The Comforting Whirlwind: God, Job and the Scale of Creation* (Cambridge: Cowley, 2005), 26; "The Comforting Whirlwind, God and the Environmental Crisis," Sermon by Bill McKibben, Delivered at the First Religious Society, Unitarian-Universalist, Carlisle, Massachusetts, March 18, 2001.
17 Paul Hawken, *Blessed Unrest* (New York: Viking, 2007), 184-189.
18 Marshall Sahlins, *The Use and Abuse of Biology* (Ann Arbor: University of Michigan Press, 1976), 100.
19 Frans de Waal, *The Age of Empathy: Nature's Lessons for a Kinder Society* (New York: Harmony Books, 2009), 207.
20 Sarah Blaffer Hrdy, *Mothers and Others: The Evolutionary Origins of Mutual Understanding* (Cambridge: Belknap Press, 2009), 4.
21 Ibid., 21, 23.
22 Ibid., 79, 78.
23 Ibid., 77. Documented in the Human Relations Area Files. Citing Barry Hewlett, *Diverse Contexts of Human Infancy* (Englewood Cliffs: Prentice Hall, 1989).
24 Ibid., 178-179.
25 Ibid., 28.
26 Richard Wilkinson and Kate Pickett, *The Spirit Level: Why More Equal Societies Almost Always Do Better* (London: Allen Lane-Penguin, 2009), 204-205.
27 Michael Gurven, "To Give or Not to Give: The Behavioral Ecology of Food Transfers," *Behavioral and Brain Sciences* 27 (2004): 543-583.
28 Michael Alvard, "Good Hunters Keep Smaller Shares of Larger Pies," Open Peer Commentary, accompanying Michael Gurven, "To Give or Not to Give: The Behavioral Ecology of Food Transfers," *Behavioral and Brain Sciences* 27 (2004): 543-583.
29 Hrdy, op.cit., 20.
30 Adam Smith, *The Theory of Moral Sentiments*, ed. D.D. Raphael and A.L. Macfie (Indianapolis: Liberty Classics, 1982), pt. 2, sec. 2, ch. 3, 88.
31 Charles R. Darwin, *The Descent of Man and Selection in Relation to Sex* (New York: D. Appleton, 1909), pt. 1, ch. 4, 121.
32 Daniel Goleman, *Social Intelligence: The New Science of Human Relationships* (New York: Bantam, 2006), 57.
33 Ibid., 55.
34 Natalie Angier, "Why We're So Nice: We're Wired to Cooperate," *New York Times*, July 23, 2002.
35 Sandra Blakeslee, "Cells that Read Minds," *New York Times*, January 10, 2006, http://www.nytimes.com/2006/01/10/science/10mirr.html.
36 Elsa Youngsteadt, "The Secret to Happiness? Giving," *ScienceNOW*, March 20, 2008, 2.
37 Michael Tomasello, *Why We Cooperate* (Cambridge: A Boston Review Book, MIT Press, 2009), ch. 2, From Social Interaction to Social Institutions, 49ff.
38 Ibid., pt. 2, sec. 2, ch. 1, 80.
39 Sarah F. Brosnan and Frans B.M. de Waal, "Monkeys Reject Unequal Pay," *Nature* 423 (2003): 297-299.
40 Martin A. Nowak, Karen M. Page, and Karl Sigmund. "Fairness versus Reason in the Ultimatum Game," *Science* 289, no. 5485 (2000): 1773.
41 Erich Fromm, *The Anatomy of Human Destructiveness* (New York: Holt, Rinehart and Winston, 1973), 264.
42 Drake Bennett, "The Upside of 'Down With': Protesters' Secret: They're Out There Because It Makes Them Happier," *Boston Globe*, October 11, 2009.
43 Christopher R. Browning, *Ordinary Men: Reserve Police Battalion 101 and the Final Solution in Poland* (Harper Perennial, 1998; first published 1992), xv.
44 Ibid., xvii, 38.
45 Ibid., xv, 47.
46 Ibid., 225-26.
47 Ibid., 184-85.
48 Philip G. Zimbardo, "A Situationist Perspective on the Psychology of Evil: Understanding How Good People Are Transformed into Perpetrators," in *The Social Psychology of Good* and

*Evil: Understanding our Capacity for Kindness and Cruelty*, ed. Arthur Miller (New York: Guilford, 2004, revised July 25, 2003), 21-50.

49 Dana Milbank and Justin Blum, "Document Says Oil Chiefs Met With Cheney Task Force," *Washington Post*, November 16, 2005, http://www.washingtonpost.com/wp-dyn/content/article/2005/11/15/AR2005111501842.html.

50 Ken Silverstein, "The Sweat of his Labor: Kristoff and the Global Apparel Industry," *Harper's Magazine*, December 17, 2009, http://harpers.org/archive/2009/12/hbc-90006262.

51 Benedict Carey, "Study Links Punishment to an Ability to Profit," *New York Times*, April 7, 2006, http://www.nytimes.com/2006/04/07/science/07punish.html?_r=1.

52 U.S. Department of State, *Trafficking in Persons Report 2009* (Washington DC: Department of State, 2009), 8, http://www.state.gov/documents/organization/123357.pdf.

53 Industry Note-Equity Strategy, "Plutonomy: Buying Luxury, Explaining Global Imbalance," Citigroup Research, a division of Citigroup Global Markets Inc., October 16, 2005, 3, http://www.scribd.com/doc/6674234/Citigroup-Oct-16-2005-Plutonomy-Report-Part-1.

54 J. S. Hacker, *The Great Risk Shift: The New Insecurity and the Decline of the American Dream* (New York: Oxford University Press, 2006).

55 Erich Fromm, *The Anatomy of Human Destructiveness* (New York: Holt, Rinehart and Winston, 1973), 149.

56 Jack Healy, "Number of Homeowners Facing Foreclosure," *New York Times*, May 28, 2009, http://www.nytimes.com/2009/05/29/business/economy/29home.html.

57 Andrew Newberg and Mark Robert Waldman, *Why We Believe What We Believe: Uncovering Our Biological Need for Meaning, Spirituality, and Truth* (New York: Free Press, 2006), 8-9; Michael Bratton and Wonbin Cho, "Where is Africa Going? Views from Below, A Compendium of Trends in Public Opinion in 12 African Countries, 1999-2006," Working Paper No. 60, The Afrobarometer Network, May 2006, 17, http://www.washingtonpost.com/wp-srv/world/documents/AfropaperNo60.pdf.

58 Howard Schneider, "Greenspan: Regret Over this 'Credit Tsunami', Former Fed Chairman Alan Greenspan Took Some Blame for the Crisis and Predicted More Turmoil," *Star Tribune*, October 23, 2008, http://www.startribune.com/business/33196929.html; "Greenspan Testimony on Sources of Financial Crisis," *Wall Street Journal*, October 23, 2008, http://blogs.wsj.com/economics/2008/10/23/greenspan-testimony-on-sources-of-financial-crisis/.

59 Peter S. Goodman, "The Reckoning: Taking Hard New Look at a Greenspan Legacy," *New York Times*, October 10, 2008, http://www.nytimes.com/2008/10/09/business/economy/09greenspan.html?_r=1&dbk=&pagewanted=print.

60 President Franklin Delano Roosevelt, Speech to Congress About the Dangers of Monopoly, April 29, 1938, http://www.presidency.ucsb.edu/ws/index.php?pid=15637.

61 Sara J. Scherr and Sajal Sthapit, "Mitigating Climate Change Through Food and Land Use," *Worldwatch Report* 179, (2009), 16.

62 Catherine Badgley, "Organic Agriculture and the Global Food Supply, "*Renewable Agriculture and Food Systems* 22 (2007): 86-108.

63 Public Policy Polling, *Obama's Approval Increases*, Public Opinion Poll, August 19, 2009.

64 Thomas Frank, *The Wrecking Crew: How Conservatives Rule* (New York: Henry Holt, 2008), 130.

65 Robert Reich, *Supercapitalism: The Transformation of Business, Democracy, and Everyday Life* (New York: Knopf, 2007), 48.

66 Jonathan Weisman, "Gloom Spreads on Economy, but GOP Doesn't Gain," *Wall Street Journal*, October 28, 2009, http://online.wsj.com/article/SB125667589615011225.html?mod=WSJ_hps_MIDDLESecondNews.

67 Robert Reich, 113. Estimates are from 2005.

68 National Opinion Research Center General Social Surveys Database, 1972-2006, http://www.norc.org/GSS+Website/Browse+GSS+Variables/Subject+Index/(for trends of variable Trust: Can People be Trusted, accessed December 19, 2009).

69 Lewis F. Powell Jr., "Confidential Memorandum: Attack of American Free Enterprise System," August 23, 1971, reproduced as "The Powell Memo," ReclaimDemocracy, April 3, 2004, http://www.reclaimdemocracy.org/corporate_accountability/powell_memo_lewis.html.

70 Ralph Nader, *Unsafe at Any Speed: The Designed-In Dangers of the American Automobile* (New York: Grossman, 1965).
71 David Callahan, *$1 Billion for Ideas: Conservative Think Tanks in the 1990s* (Washington, DC: National Committee for Responsive Philanthropy, 1999).
72 "About Campus Progress," Center for American Progress, http://www.campusprogress.org/about (accessed on March 8, 2005); Ben Hubbard (Campus Programs Director), Personal Communication, March 7, 2005. Estimate of $35 million is based on the 2003 IRS Form 990s of the top twelve conservative youth development organizations, such as Young America's Foundation, the Leadership Institute, and the Intercollegiate Studies Institute. The additional tens of millions of dollars go toward endowing professorships, chairs, academic centers and programs, and scholarships for graduate study.
73 David Brock, *The Republican Noise Machine* (New York: Crown, 2004), 380.
74 National Sheriff's Association, Alexandria, Va., cited in Harper's Index, *Harper's Magazine*, January 2010, 11, http://harpers.org/archive/2010/01/page/0013.
75 Jeffrey Gold, "Wal-Mart, Toys 'R' Us Rivalry 'a Little More Cutthroat," *Seattle Post-Intelligencer*, November 23, 2003, Business section, http://www.seattlepi.com/business/150216_toyshowdown28.html.
76 Peter Barnes, *Capitalism 3.0* (San Francisco: Berrett-Koehler, 2006), 22. Calculated from annual sales of Fortune 500 corporations from data on *Fortune* magazine's Website, http://money.cnn.com/magazines/fortune/fortune500_archive/full/1955/index.html.
77 Emmanuel Saez, "Striking it Richer: The Evolution of Top Incomes in the United States Update with 2007 Estimates," Working paper, Department of Economics, University of California, Berkeley, 2009; Office for Social Justice, Archdiocese of St. Paul and Minneapolis, based on Census Bureau figures and analysis by Princeton economist Paul Krugman, http://www.osjspm.org/101_income_facts. aspx#6.
78 Emmanuel Saez, "Striking it Richer: The Evolution of Top Incomes in the United States Update with 2007 Estimates," Working paper, Department of Economics, University of California, Berkeley, 2009.
79 Associated Press, "Labor Department: Worker Productivity Rises Most in 6 Years," *New York Daily News*, September 2, 2009, http://www.nydailynews.com/money/work_career/2009/09/02/2009-09-02_and_were_working_even_harder_now_worker_productivity_rises_most_in_6_years_.html#ixzz0ZPJsHwUU.
80 "CEO Pay Charts," United for a Fair Economy, http://www.faireconomy.org/news/ceo_pay_charts (accessed on January 3, 2007); For information on CEO "lunchtime" comparison: Bob Herbert, "Working for a Pittance," *New York Times*, July 3, 2006, citing the Economic Policy Institute, Washington, DC.
81 Central Intelligence Agency, *The World Factbook 2009* (Washington, DC: Central Intelligence Agency, 2009), https://www.cia.gov/library/publications/the-world-factbook/fields/2172.html.
82 Matthew Miller and Duncan Greenberg, eds., "The Forbes 400," *Forbes*, September 30, 2009, http://www.forbes.com/2009/09/29/forbes-400-buffett-gates-ellison-rich-list-09-intro.html. Global household wealth (defined as the value of physical and financial assets minus debts) in 2000 was valued at $125 trillion, according to The World Distribution of Household Wealth Report (Davies, Sandstrom, Shorrocks & Wolff, Department of Economics, University of Western Ontario, London, Canada, December 5, 2006). According to the same study, and reported at www.freelibrary.com, 50 percent of the world's adults owned barely 1 percent of global wealth, which would equal $1.25 trillion.
83 Industry Note-Equity Strategy, "Plutonomy: Buying Luxury, Explaining Global Imbalance," Citigroup Research, a division of Citigroup Global Markets Inc., October 16, 2005, 1-2, http://www.scribd.com/doc/6674234/Citigroup-Oct-16-2005-Plutonomy-Report-Part-1.
84 David Woodward and Andrew Sims, "Growth Isn't Working: the Unbalanced Distribution of Benefits and Costs from Economic Growth," The New Economics Foundation, January, 2006, 3, 17, http://www.neweconomics.org/sites/neweconomics.org/files/Growth_Isnt_Working_1.pdf.
85 Food and Agriculture Organization of the United Nations, "One Sixth of Humanity Undernourished—More Than Ever Before," http://www.fao.org/news/story/en/item/20568/icode/.

86 "A Survey of the World Economy: More Pain than Gain," *The Economist*, September 14, 2006, 15.
87 Jeffrey Sachs, *The End of Poverty* (New York: The Penguin Press, 2005).
88 Thomas Geoghegan, "Infinite Debt: How Unlimited Interest Rates Destroyed the Economy," *Harper's Magazine*, April 2009, 33.
89 For facts on the grain trade, see: Bill Vorley, Food Inc.: *Corporate Concentration from Farm to Consumer* (London: U.K. Food Group), 11; For seed facts, see: "Global Seed Industry Concentration 2005," Communiqué Issue 90, ETC Group, September-October, 2005, 3; For media facts, see: Ben Bagdikian, *The New Media Monopoly* (Boston: Beacon Press, 2004); See also: Granville Williams, "Bestriding the World," http://www.mediachannel.org/ownership/granville.shtml; For gasoline facts, see: Public Citizen, *Mergers, Manipulation and Mirages: How Oil Companies Keep Gasoline Prices High, and Why the Energy Bill Doesn't Help*, March 2004, http://www.citizen.org/documents/oilmergers.pdf; For information on Intel, see: *New York Times*, "Big Food," Editorial, January 25, 2010.
90 "Figuring Out What's in Your Food," *CBS Evening News*, May 11, 2008, http://www.cbsnews.com/stories/2008/05/11/eveningnews/main4086518.shtml; Guillaume P. Gruère and S.R. Rao, "A Review of International Labeling Policies of Genetically Modified Food to Evaluate India's Proposed Rule," *Journal of Agrobiotechnology Management and Economics* 10, no. 1 (2007), http://www.agbioforum.org/v10n1/v10n1a06-gruere.htm.
91 *New York Times*, "Even Bigger Than Too Big to Fail," Editorial, December 14, 2009, http://www.nytimes.com/2009/12/15/opinion/15tue1.html?_r=1.
92 David Cho, "Banks 'Too Big to Fail' Have Grown Even Bigger," *Washington Post*, August 28, 2009, http://www.washingtonpost.com/wp-dyn/content/article/2009/08/27/AR2009082704193.html?sid=ST2009090801107.
93 Paul Krugman, "The Great Wealth Transfer," *Rolling Stone*, November 30, 2006, http://www.rollingstone.com/politics/story/12699486/paul_krugman_on_the_great_wealth_transfer.
94 Reich, op. cit., 106.
95 Office for Social Justice, Archdiocese of St. Paul and Minneapolis, based on Lawrence Mishel, et al., *The State of Working America 2002/2003*, (Washington DC: The Economic Policy Institute, 2003), http://www.osjspm.org/101_income_facts.aspx#7.
96 Center for Responsive Politics, "Lobbying Database," http://www.opensecrets.org/lobby/index.php (accessed on December 22, 2009).
97 *New York Times*, "Really Big Money Politics," Editorial, January 3, 2010, http://www.nytimes.com/2010/01/04/opinion/04mon4.html.
98 Simon Johnson, Interview by Bill Moyers, *Bill Moyers Journal*, PBS, October 9, 2009, http://www.pbs.org/moyers/journal/10092009/transcript4.html.
99 Michael Hirsh, "Why is Barney Frank so Effing Mad?," *Newsweek*, December 5, 2009, http://www.newsweek.com/id/225781.
100 Matt Taibbi and Robert Kutner, Interview by Bill Moyers, *Bill Moyers Journal*, PBS, December 18, 2009.
101 Americans for Financial Reform, "Wall St. Bonuses Could Fund an Economic Recovery for Millions of Americans," December 17, 2009, http://ourfinancialsecurity.org/2009/12/wall-street-bonuses-could-fund-an-economic-recovery-for-millions-of-americans/.
102 Senator Dick Durbin, quoted in Joe Weisenthal, "Senator Admits That Bankers Own Capitol Hill," The Business Insider, May 1, 2009, http://www.businessinsider.com/senator-admits-that-bankers-own-capitol-hill-2009-5.
103 For information on lobbying, see: Harper's Index, *Harper's Magazine*, January, 2010, citing Center for Responsive Politics, 11; For information on deaths of the uninsured, see: Susan Heavey, "Study Links 45,000 U.S. Deaths to Lack of Insurance," September 17, 2009, http://www.reuters.com/article/idUSTRE58G6W520090917.
104 Central Intelligence Agency, *World Fact Book 2009* (Washington, DC: Central Intelligence Agency, 2009), https://www.cia.gov/library/publications/the-world-factbook/rankorder/2091rank.html?countryName=United%20States&countryCode=us®ionCode=na&rank=180#top (accessed on December 22, 2009).

105 Asian Development Bank, "Global Financial Market Losses Reach $50 Trillion, Says Study," Press Release, March 9, 2009, http://www.adb.org/Media/Articles/2009/12818-global-financial-crisis/.
106 Associated Press, "U.S. Food Safety Inspections Languishing," February 26, 2007, http://fsrio.nal.usda.gov/news_article.php?article_id=4110.
107 Patrice Woeppel, Interview by Robin Young, *Here & Now*, National Public Radio, December 9, 2009; For more information, see: Patrice Woeppel, *Depraved Indifference* (Bloomington: iUniverse, 2008).
108 "Large Majorities Believe Big Companies, PACs, Media and Lobbyists Have Too Much Power and Influence in Washington," Harris Interactive, March 12, 2009, http://www.harrisinteractive.com/harris_poll/pubs/Harris_Poll_2009_03_12.pdf.
109 Ori Brafman and Rod Beckstrom, *The Starfish and the Spider* (New York: Portfolio, 2007), 17-22.
110 Reuters, "Healthcare shares rise as US reform bill progresses," December 21, 2009, http://www.reuters.com/article/idUSN2123614720091221.
111 Richard Wilkinson and Kate Pickett, *The Spirit Level: Why More Equal Societies Almost Always Do Better* (London: Allan Lane-Penguin, 2009), 75.
112 Ibid., 174, 193.
113 Miller, op. cit.
114 Sarah Anderson et al., "Executive Excess 2006: Defense and Oil Executives Cash in on Conflict," United for a Fair Economy, August 30, 2006, 5, http://www.faireconomy.org/files/pdf/ExecutiveExcess2006.pdf.
115 Jerry Markon, "Pakistan Arrests 5 North Virginia Men, Probes Possible Jihadist Ties," *Washington Post*, December 10, 2009, http://www.washingtonpost.com/wp-dyn/content/article/2009/12/09/AR2009120901884.html.
116 Laura Yuen, "Feds Indict Minnesota Somali on Conspiracy Charges," *Minnesota Public Radio*, November 19, 2009, http://minnesota.publicradio.org/display/web/2009/11/19/somali-recruiter-charges/.
117 Sandra Jordan, "Old Women Step Forward as 'Martyrs,'" *The Observer*, December 12, 2006, 27.
118 Beatriz Stolowicz, "The Latin American Left: Between Governability and Change," in *The Left in the City*, eds. Daniel Chavez and Benjamin Goldfrank (London: Latin American Bureau, 2004), citing *Desarrollo Más Allá de la Economía*, Inter-American Development Bank, September 2000, 180.
119 Alexei Barrionuevo, "Chile's Children of Democracy Sitting Out Presidential Election," *The New York Times*, December 12, 2009.
120 Richard D. Wolff, *Capitalism Hits the Wall: The Global Economic Meltdown and What We Can Do About It* (Northampton, Ma.: Olive Branch Press, 2010), 125.
121 John Halpin and others, *The Structural Imbalance of Political Talk Radio* (Washington DC: Center for American Progress and Free Press, 2007), http://www.americanprogress.org/issues/2007/06/talk_radio.html.
122 "Progressive Values Dominant—But Need to Rebuild Trust in Effectiveness of Government Action," Progressive States Network, November 2009, drawing on Pew Research Center for the People and the Press, "Trends in Political Values and Core Attitudes: 1987-2009," and Center for American Progress, "State of American Political Ideology, 2009: A National Study of Values and Beliefs," http://www.progressivestates.org/node/23897.
123 Albert Camus, *Neither Victims Nor Executioners* (Boston: New Society Publishers, 1986), 49.
124 Thomas L. Friedman, "Time of the Turtles," *New York Times*, August 15, 1998, A13.
125 John Keane, *The Life and Death of Democracy* (New York: Simon and Schuster, 2009), 852.
126 Barry Lopez, "Imperative," *Orion*, January/February 2007, 39.
127 Stephen Breyer, *Active Liberty* (New York: Alfred Knopf, 2005), 21.
128 John J. Dinan, *The American State Constitutional Tradition* (Lawrence: University Press of Kansas, 2006), 1.
129 William H. Hastie, quoted in *The Great Quotations*, ed. George Seldes (New York: Pocketbooks, 1967), 265.
130 Gianpaolo Baiocchi, "Participation, Activism, and Politics: The Porto Alegre Experiment,"

in *Deepening Democracy*, ed. Archon Fung and Erik Olin Wright (New York: Verso, 2003), 47-50.

131 Gianpaolo Baiocchi, "Porto Alegre: The Dynamism of the Unorganized," in *The Left in the City*, ed. Daniel Chavez and Benjamin Goldfrank (London: Latin American Bureau, 2004), 53.

132 Gianpaolo Baiocchi, *Militants and Citizens: The Politics of Participation in Porto Alegre* (Stanford, CA: Stanford University Press, 2005); Gianpaolo Baiocchi, Personal Communication, March 11, 2005.

133 Tiago Peixoto, "From Australia, an E-Participatory Budgeting Experiment," http://www.participatorybudgeting.org/.

134 *The Very Separate World of Conservative Republicans*, Carville Greenberg Democracy Corps, Greenberg, Quinlan, Rosner Research, October 16, 2009, 2, http://www.greenbergresearch.com/articles/2398/5488_TheVerySeparateWorldofConservativeRepublicans101609.pdf.

135 Project Quest, "History," http://www.questsa.org/About/History.html (accessed on December 22, 2009).

136 "Shared Decision Making at a School Site: Moving Toward a Professional Model," *American Educator* (Spring, 1987): 17.

137 Herman Scheer, *Energy Autonomy* (London, Sterling, VA: Earthscan, 2007), 48; Cristina L. Archer and Mark Z. Jacobson, "Evaluation of Global Wind Power," *Journal of Geophysical Research*, Vol. 110, D121 10, June 30, 2005, 1. http://www.stanford.edu/group/efmh/winds/2004jd005462.pdf.

138 Paul Hawken, Amory Lovins, and L. Hunter Lovins, *Natural Capitalism* (Boston, New York, London: Little Brown and Company, 1999), 14-15.

139 Michael McDonald, "2008 General Election Turnout Rates," The United States Election Project, George Mason University, http://elections.gmu.edu/Turnout_2008G.html; Michael McDonald, "2000 General Election Turnout Rates," The United States Election Project, George Mason University, http://elections.gmu.edu/Turnout_2000G.html.

140 Micah L. Sifry and Nancy Watzman, *Is That a Politician in Your Pocket? Washington on $2 Million a Day* (Hoboken, NJ: Wiley, 2004), 19.

141 Thomas L. Friedman, "The Power of Green," *New York Times Magazine*, April 15, 2007, 71.

142 U.S. Census Bureau, *Income, Poverty, and Health Insurance Coverage in the United States: 2008* (Washington, DC: GPO, 2009), 13.

143 For information on children dependent on food stamps, see: Mark Rank, professor of social welfare, Washington University, St. Louis, cited in Harper's Index, *Harper's Magazine*, February, 2010; For prison estimates, see: Michael Myser, "The Hard Sell," CNN Business Magazine 2.0, March 15, 2007, http://money.cnn.com/magazines/business2/business2_archive/2006/12/01/8394995/index.htm; James J. Stephen, "State Prison Expenditures, 2001," 3, http://www. ojp.usdoj.gov/bjs/pub/pdf/spe01.pdf; For Harvard tuition 2001-2002, see: http://www.hsph.harvard.edu/ finaid/01-02budget.shtml.

144 Harry J. Holzer et al., *The Economic Costs of Poverty in the United States: Subsequent Effects of Children Growing Up Poor* (Washington, DC: Center for American Progress, January 2007), 1, http://www.americanprogress.org/issues/2007/01/pdf/poverty_report.pdf; For the estimate of "four in ten," see: National Center for Children in Poverty, Columbia University, 2009, http://www.nccp.org/topics/childpoverty.html.

145 U.S. Environmental Protection Agency, Office of Solid Waste and Emergency Response, Technology Innovation Office, *Cleaning Up the Nation's Waste Sites: Markets and Technology Trends*, (Washington, DC: EPA, September 2004), http://www.clu-in.org/download/market/2004market.pdf.

146 "Climate Change Fight 'can't wait'," BBC News, October 31, 2006, http://news.bbc.co.uk/2/hi/6096084.stm#top.

147 "From Poverty to Prosperity," 8-9.

148 Dan Ackman, "Corporate Taxes Continue to Plummet," first published by Forbes.com, September 23, 2004.

149 Harper's Index, *Harper's Magazine*, February, 2010.

150 Paul Krugman, "Gilded Once More," *New York Times*, April 27, 2007, A27.

151 Adam Smith, *The Wealth of Nations* (New York: Random House, 1937), bk. 5, ch. 2, pt. 2,

777.

152 Lester Brown, *Plan B2.0* (New York: W.W. Norton, 2006), 228-235.

153 "From Poverty to Prosperity," 5.

154 Electronics TakeBack Coalition, "State Legislation," http://www.computertakeback.com/legislation/state_legislation.htm; Sam Cole, "Zero Waste—On the Move Around the World: U.S. Communities, Retailers, and Other Countries Begin to Implement Producer Responsibility," Eco-Cycle, www.ecocycle.org/zero/producer.cfm.

155 Lester Brown, *Plan B2.0* (New York: W.W. Norton, 2006), 229.

156 Congressional Budget Office, "Designing a Premium Support System for Medicare," November 2006, 12, http://www.gao.gov/new.items/d09132r.pdf; Congressional Budget Office, "Key Issues in Analyzing Major Health Insurance Proposals," December 2008, 92, http://www.cbo.gov/ftpdocs/99xx/doc9924/12-18-KeyIssues.pdf.

157 Greg Anrig, Jr., "Ten Myths about Social Security," The Century Foundation, January 26, 2005, http://www.tcf.org/Publications/RetirementSecurity/10myths1-25-05.pdf.

158 France spends $3,159 per person with a life expectancy of 80.3 years, and the U.S. spent $6,102 per person in 2004 on health care with a life expectancy of 78 years. "OECD in Figures 2006-2007: Health Spending and Resources," Organization for Economic Cooperation and Development, October, 2006, http://www.oecd.org/LongAbstract/0,3425,en_2825_499395_35672488_1_1_1_1,00.html; Martin Gaynor and Deepti Gudipati, "Health Care Costs: Do We Need a Cure," *The Heinz School Review* 3, no. 2 (2006).

159 EverBank, "Norway Economic Information," http://www.everbank.com/002CurrencyNorway.aspx (accessed January 5, 2010); Aasa Christine Stoltz and Wojchiech Moskwa, "Norway Sees Unemployment Rising in 2009 and 2010," *Thomson Financial News*, March 10, 2009, http://www.forbes.com/feeds/afx/2009/03/10/afx6145709.html; Andrew Clark, "US Employment Rate Surges to Worst Since 1983," *Guardian*, March 6, 2009, http://www.guardian.co.uk/business/2009/mar/06/us-unemployment-rate-jobs.

160 Xavier Gabaix and Augustin Landier, "Why Has CEO Pay Increased So Much?" *Quarterly Journal of Economics*, April 9, 2007, 2, http://pages.stern.nyu.edu/~alandier/pdfs/CEO.pdf; In 1980, the minimum wage was $3.10. See U.S. Department of Labor table: http://www.dol.gov/whd/state/stateMinWageHis.htm.

161 These programs I learned about firsthand from the program's director Adriana Aranha on my visit to Belo Horizonte in 2000. The specifics of forty farmers and twelve thousand meals daily come from an email communication dated July 6, 2006, from Michael Jahi Chappell, mjahi@umich.edu, doctoral candidate at the University of Michigan studying Belo Horizonte.

162 Dr. Maja Göpel, *Celebrating the Belo Horizonte Food Security Programme: Future Policy Award 2009 Solutions for the Food Crisis* (Hamburg: World Future Council, 2009), 5.

163 Ibid., Estimate of cost per resident by the author, drawn from data in: Michael Jahi Chappell, "From Food Security to Farm to Formicidae: Belo Horizonte, Brazil's Secretaria Municipal de Abastecimento and Biodiversity in the Fragmented Atlantic Rainforest," Doctoral dissertation, Department of Ecology and Evolutionary Biology, University of Michigan, 2009.

*164 2007 Report on Socially Responsible Investing Trends in the United States,* Executive Summary (Washington, DC: Social Investment Forum Foundation, 2007), ii.

165 See CERES, the twenty-year-old coalition that launched the Global Reporting Initiative (GRI), the de facto international standard used by over 850 companies for corporate reporting on environmental, social, and economic performance, http://www.ceres.org; See also: http://www.globalreporting.org.

166 Coco McCabe, "U.S. Farmworkers Reach Historic Agreement with McDonald's," Oxfam America, April 10, 2007, http://www.oxfamamerica.org/articles/us-farmworkers-reach-historic-agreement-with-mcdonalds; McDonald's Campaign Archive, "Shareholder Resolution Calling for Human Rights Protections in McD's Supply Chain Moves Forward Following SEC Ruling," Coalition of Immokale Workers, http://www.ciw-online.org/McDonald%27s_campaign_archive.html.

167 Fairtrade Labeling Organizations International, "Facts and Figures," http://www.fairtrade.net/facts_and_figures.html (accessed December 4, 2009).

168 TransFair USA, "Fair Trade Certified—Frequently Asked Questions," http://www.transfairusa.org/content/resources/faq.php (accessed December 4, 2009).

169 Corporate Accountability International, http://www.stopcorporateabuse.org/cms/page1111.cfm; See also: http://www.stopcorporateabuse.org/global-tobacco-treaty-background.

170 "A Billion Will Die from Smoking," BBC News, October 4, 2005, quoting Professor Richard Peto, Oxford University, Oxford, England, http://news.bbc.co.uk/2/hi/health/4309222.stm.

171 Jack Beatty, *Age of Betrayal: The Triumph of Money in America, 1865-1900* (New York: Alfred A. Knopf, 2007), 148.

172 General facts from personal communication with the Community Environmental Legal Defense Fund, January, 2010; For facts about Blaine County, see: "Pennsylvania Township Becomes First in Nation to Ban Mining," Press Release, http://www.celdf.org/PressReleases/PATownshipFirstToBanCorporationsFromMining/tabid/375/Default.aspx.

173 "Signs of Life, Maine Towns Fight Back," *Yes! Magazine*, Summer, 2009, 6-7.

174 Community Environmental Defense Fund, http://www.celdf.org/PressReleases//EastBrunswickStripsSludgeCorporationsofRigh/tabid/407/Default.aspx; Democracy Unlimited of Humboldt County, http://www.duhc.org/index.html.

175 Daniel McLeod, "Ballot Initiative, Democracy Unlimited: Daniel McLeod Interviews Kaitlin Sopoci-Belknap," December 2006, http://www.localdemocracy.org/publications/z_magazine_measure_t.

176 Kaitlin Sopoci-Belknap, "Humboldt County Board of Supervisors Cave to Corporate Pressure: Agreement to Settle Over Measure T Filed in Federal Court," Yes on Measure T, Humbolt County Coalition for Community Rights, November 10, 2008, http://www.votelocalcontrol.org/news_HCCR_PR111008.htm.

177 Marjorie Kelly, "Holy Grail Found: Absolute, Definitive Proof That Responsible Companies Perform Better Financially," *Business Ethics*, Winter 2005, http://www.business-ethics.com/current_issue/ winter_2005_holy_grail_article.html.

178 Andrew W. Savitz, *The Triple Bottom Line* (San Francisco: Jossey-Bass, 2006), 31.

179 Francesco Guerrera, "GE Wins $1.4 Billion Wind Turbine Deal," *Financial Times*, December 10, 2009, http://www.ft.com/cms/s/0/4d5ea0bc-e5f4-11de-b5d7-00144feab49a.html?nclick_check=1; General Electric, "GE's Energy's 1.5 Megawatt Wind Turbine Maintains Top Spot in U.S. Wind Industry," Press Release, May 4, 2009, http://www.gepower.com/about/press/en/2009_press/050409c.htm.

180 John Doerr and Jeff Immelt, "Falling Behind on Green Tech," *Washington Post*, August 3, 2009, http://www.washingtonpost.com/wp-dyn/content/article/2009/08/02/AR2009080201563.html.

181 Daniel Gross, "Latte Laborers Take on a Latte-Liberal Business," *New York Times*, April 8, 2007, Week in Review, 5.

182 Diane Bartz, "Whole Foods, FTC Settle on Wild Oats Merger," Reuters, March 6, 2009, http://www.reuters.com/article/innovationNews/idUSTRE5253AL20090306.

183 "Unchaining for One Day Means Millions for Communities," American Independent Business Alliance, November 10, 2004, http://amiba.net/Unchained_national_release.html citing "The Economic Impact of Locally Owned Businesses vs. Chains: A Case Study in Midcoast Maine," Institute for Local Self-Reliance, September 2003, http://www.newrules.org/sites/newrules.org/files/midcoaststudy.pdf.

184 For news of Bellingham and the local living economies movement, www.livingeconomies.org.

185 Stacey Mitchell, "Voters Reject Massive Big-Box Complex in Mendocino County, California," New Rules Project, November 9, 2009, http://www.newrules.org/retail/news/voters-reject-massive-bigbox-complex-mendocino-county-california; With updated statistics in email to author from campaign participant Sheilah Rogers in Ukiah.

186 Michael Shuman, "Local Stock Exchanges and National Stimulus," (citing Statistical Abstract data), Small-Mart Revolution, http://small-mart.org/local-exchanges-as-national-stimulus.

187 The logic of this estimate: The International Cooperative Alliance reports 800 million cooperative members worldwide. Considering the combined population of the EU and the U.S.

is less than this number, and assuming that at the very most half of the people in these two regions own corporate shares, one can assume as many as several hundred additional million shareholders in the rest of the world and still arrive at less than 800 million.

188 *ICA Digest*, International Cooperative Alliance, March 2007, 5, Issue 54, http://www.ica.coop/ publications/digest/54-digest.pdf; World Economic Forum, Global Competitive Report 2009-2010, http://www.ica.coop/publications/digest/54-digest.pdf.

189 Examples, except where otherwise noted, are from International Cooperative Alliance except for India, which is from: *Cooperatives in Social Development*, Report of the Secretary-General, United Nations General Assembly, A/60/138, July 21, 2005, 6, citing Kurien Verghese, "India's Milk Revolution: Investing in rural producer organizations," A paper presented at the World Bank conference "Scaling Up Poverty Reduction: A global learning process and conference," Shanghai, May 25-27, 2004; For data on the number of owners, see: National Dairy Development Board, "Facts at a Glance," http://www.nddb.org/achievement/ataglance.html (accessed December 11, 2009).

190 National Dairy Development Board, "Facts at a Glance," http://www.nddb.org/achievement/ataglance.html, (accessed December 23, 2009).

191 Sara Sidner, "Odd Jobs Run India's Economy," CNN News, October 14, 2009, http://edition.cnn.com/2009/BUSINESS/10/14/india.informal.economy/index.html.

192 Jaisal Noor, "Worker-Run Businesses Flourish in Argentina," *Indypendent*, August 14, 2009, http://www.indypendent.org/2009/08/13/worker-run-businesses/.

193 Stacey Hannah, Personal Email Message, December 10, 2009.

194 KIDS Consortium, Brandeis University, "Center for Youth and Communities' study, 2004-2006-The Evidence," http://www.kidsconsortium.org/evidence.php.

195 "WRC Affiliated Colleges and Universities," Workers Rights Consortium, http://www.workersrights.org/about/as.asp.

196 Steven Greenhouse, "Labor Fight Ends with Win for Students," *New York Times*, November 17, 2009, http://www.nytimes.com/2009/11/18/business/18labor.html?_r=2.

197 Gordon Bazemore and Maria Schiff, *Juvenile Justice Reform and Restorative Justice: Building Theory and Policy from Practice* (Portland, OR: Willan Publishing, 2004), 376-378.

198 Citizens On Patrol Program (COPP), http://www.cincinnati-oh.gov/police/pages/-9496-/; *Citizen Observer*, http://www.citizenobserver.com/cov6/app/group.html?id=174.

199 Jim Giles, "Internet Encyclopedias Go Head to Head," *Nature* 438 (December 15, 2005): 900ff.

200 Richard Stallman, "Lest CodePlex Perplex," Free Software Foundation, http://www.fsf.org/blogs/rms.

201 Alasdair Roberts, *Blacked Out: Government Secrecy in the Information Age* (New York: Cambridge University Press, 2006), 73.

202 Archon Fung and Dara O'Rourke, "Reinventing Environmental Regulation from the Grassroots Up: Explaining and Expanding the Success of the Toxics Release Inventory," *Environmental Management* 25, no. 2 (2000): 115, http://www.archonfung.net/papers/FungORourkeTRI00.pdf; Andrew W. Savitz with Karl Weber, *The Triple Bottom Line* (San Francisco: Jossey-Bass, 2006), 210.

203 Indymedia, "Frequently Asked Questions," http://docs.indymedia.org/view/Global/FrequentlyAskedQuestions (accessed on December 27, 2009).

204 United Nations Development Programme 2002, *Human Development Report 2002* (New York: Oxford University Press, 2002), 10.

205 For 12 million estimate, see: International Labour Organization, "A Global Alliance Against Forced Labor 2005-Executive Summary," http://www.ilo.org/public/english/region/asro/manila/downloads/flexsum.pdf; For estimate of 27 million and Bales, see: Susan Llewelyn Leach, "Slavery is Not Dead, Just Less Recognizable," *Christian Science Monitor*, September 1, 2004, http://www.csmonitor.com/2004/0901/p16s01-wogi.html.

206 Thomas L. Friedman, "The Power of Green," *New York Times Magazine*, April 15, 2007, 49, citing the Environmental Protection Agency.

207 *Bill Moyers Journal*, PBS, April 27, 2007.

208 Josephson Institute of Ethics, "2002 Report Card: Survey Documents Decade of Moral Deterioration: Kids Today Are More Likely to Cheat, Steal and Lie Than Kids 10 Years Ago,"

http://www.josephsoninstitute.org/Survey2002/survey2002-pressrelease.htm.
209 Daniel Goleman, *Social Intelligence: The New Science of Human Relationships* (New York: Bantam, 2006), 4, citing G. di Pelligrino et al., "Understanding Motor Events: A Neurophysiological Study," *Experimental Brain Research* 91 (1992): 176-80.
210 Daniel Goleman, *Social Intelligence: The New Science of Human Relationships* (New York: Bantam, 2006), 4.
211 For more on the arts of democracy mentioned here, see: Small Planet Institute's downloadable document: *Doing Democracy: Ten Practical Arts*, http://democracysedge.org/handbook.pdf.
212 Mark Warren, *Dry Bones Rattling: Community Building to Revitalize American Democracy,* (Princeton: Princeton University Press, 2001).
213 Benjamin Barber, "America Skips School," *Harper's Magazine*, November, 1993.
214 Dale Keiger, "The Number," *Johns Hopkins Magazine* 59, no. 1 (February 2007), http://www.jhu.edu/jhumag/0207web/number.html.
215 Jeremy Rifkin, *The European Dream: How Europe's Vision of the Future is Quietly Eclipsing the American Dream* (Cambridge: Polity Press, 2004), 48-50, 78-81.
216 Martha Meana and Lea Thaler, "Teen Sexuality and Pregnancy in Nevada," in Shalin, Dmitri, ed., *The Social Health of Nevada: Leading Indicators and Quality of Life in the Silver State* (Las Vegas: University of Nevada, 2004), http://www.unlv.edu/centers/cdclv/healthnv/teensex.html.
217 See Small Planet Institute's downloadable document: *Doing Democracy: Ten Practical Arts* http://democracysedge.org/handbook.pdf.
218 See "Suggestions for Using the Believing Game," excerpted from Gayle Mertz and Carol Miller Lieber, "Conflict in Context: Understanding Local to Global Security," Educators for Social Responsibility, 2001, http://www.esrnational.org/store/index.php?main_page=product_info&products_id=36.
219 James Surowiecki, *The Wisdom of Crowds* (New York: Doubleday, 2004), 30.
220 Nancy A. Burrell, Cindy S. Zirbel, and Mike Allen, "Evaluating Peer Mediation Outcomes in Educational Settings: A Meta-Analytic Review," 21 (2003): 7-26.
221 Ben Bagdikian, *The New Media Monopoly* (Boston: Beacon Press, 2004); See also: Granville Williams, "Bestriding the World," http://www.mediachannel.org/ownership/granville.shtml; For gasoline facts, see: Public Citizen, *Mergers, Manipulation and Mirages: How Oil Companies Keep Gasoline Prices High, and Why the Energy Bill Doesn't Help*, March 2004, http://www.citizen.org/documents/oilmergers.pdf.
222 John Halpin and others, *The Structural Imbalance of Political Talk Radio* (Washington DC: Center for American Progress and Free Press, 2007), http://www.americanprogress.org/issues/2007/06/pdf/talk_radio.pdf.
223 BBC Worldwide Poll, "Wide Dissatisfaction with Capitalism—Twenty Years after Fall of Berlin Wall," November 9, 2009, http://www.worldpublicopinion.org/pipa/articles/btglobalizationtradera/644.php?nid=&id=&pnt=644&lb=.
224 Joseph Stiglitz, *Globalization and Its Discontents* (New York: Norton, 2003), 9.
225 Thomas L. Friedman, "Small and Smaller," *New York Times*, March 4, 2004, A29.
226 Quoted in Dan Carney, "Dwayne's World," *Mother Jones*, July-August 1995, http://www.motherjones.com/news/special_reports/1995/07/carney.html.
227 "Power Hungry: Six Reasons to Regulate Global Food Corporations," Action Aid International, 2005, 4, http://www.actionaid.org.uk/wps/content/documents/power_hungry.pdf.
228 Rudyard Kipling, speaking to the Royal College of Surgeons, in London, 1923.
229 Muhammad Yunus, Personal Communication, July 2000, Dhaka, Bangladesh.
230 Associated Press, "American's Job Satisfaction Falls to Record Low," *National Public Radio*, January 5, 2010, http://www.npr.org/templates/story/story.php?storyId=122239179.
231 James Gilligan, *Violence: Reflections on a National Epidemic* (New York: Vintage Books/Random House, 1997), 105-107.
232 Eleanor Roosevelt, "Fear, the Great Enemy," in *You Learn by Living* (New York: Harper & Brothers Publishers, 1960), 29-30, 41.
233 Rush W. Dozier, Jr., *Fear Itself: The Origin and Nature of the Powerful Emotion That Shapes Our Lives and Our World* (New York: St. Martins, 1998), 224.

234 Aung San Suu Kyi, *Freedom from Fear* (New York: Penguin Books, 1991), 180.
235 Andrew Newberg, *Why We Believe What We Believe: Uncovering Our Biological Need for Meaning, Spirituality, and Truth* (New York: Free Press, 2006), 146.
236 Martha Stout, *The Sociopath Next Door* (New York: Broadway, 2005).
237 Thomas Jefferson in a Letter to Thomas Law, *Thomas Jefferson Writings*, ed. Merrill D. Peterson (New York: The Library of America/Liberty Classics, 1984), 337-338.
238 See, for example, the work of Marshall Rosenberg on "nonviolent communication," http://www.cnvc.org.
239 "Buying the War," *Bill Moyers Journal*, PBS, April 25, 2003.
240 "An Interview with Martha Stout," Book Browse, http://www.bookbrowse.com/author_interviews/. full/index.cfm?author_number=1097; Stanley Milgram, *Obedience to Authority: An Experimental View* (New York: HarperCollins, 1974).
241 Dee Hock, *Birth of the Chaordic Age* (San Francisco: Barrett-Koehler, 1999), 3.
242 Celia W. Dugger, "Even as Africa Hungers, Policy Slows Delivery of U.S. Food Aid," *New York Times*, April 7, 2007, A1, 7.
243 USDA Foreign Agricultural Service, "Fact Sheet: Food Assistance," April 2009, http://www.fas.usda.gov/info/factsheets/foodaid.asp.
244 World Health Organization, "World Health Organization Assesses the World's Health Systems," June 21, 2000, http://www.who.int/whr/2000/media_centre/press_release/en/index.html; National Center for Education Statistics, "Special Analysis 2009-International Assessments," http://nces.ed.gov/programs/coe/2009/analysis/table06.asp; For statistics on U.S. economy, see: Reich, op. cit.
245 International Data Corporation, "PC Shipments to Drop 4.5% in 2009, According to IDC," Press Release, March 5, 2009, http://www.idc.com/getdoc.jsp?containerId=prUS21725509.
246 National Resource Council of Maine, "Maine's Electronic Waste Recycling Law Huge Success," April 18, 2008, http://www.nrcm.org/news_detail.asp?news=2345.
247 Electronics Takeback Committee, "State Legislation," http://www.computertakeback.com/legislation/state_legislation.htm (accessed December 26, 2009).
248 Miguel Mendonca, *Feed-In Tariffs, Accelerating the Deployment of Renewable Energy* (London: Earthscan, 2007), 45; See also: Hermann Scheer, *Energy Autonomy* (London: Earthscan, 2007); Miguel Mendonca, David Jacobs and Benjamin Sovacool, *Powering the Green Economy–The Feed-in Tariff Handbook* (London: Earthscan, 2010).
249 Ibid. See chapters 7 and 8, 'Dispelling the Myths about Technical Issues' and 'Barriers to Renewable Energy Deployment.'
250 Peter Droege, ed., *100% Renewable* (London: Earthscan, 2009).
251 Miguel Mendonca, Personal Communication, November 25, 2009.
252 Bruce Stokes, "China Must do More on Climate Change," *National Journal Magazine*, May 30, 2009, http://www.nationaljournal.com/njmagazine/ei_20090530_1168.php.
253 BBMG, *BBMG Conscious Consumer Report: Redefining Value in a New Economy* (New York: BBGM, 2009).
254 Hardik Savalia (B Lab core team member, B Corporation), in discussion with author, September 17, 2009.
255 Co-op America Green Pages, http://www.coopamerica.org/pubs/greenpages/.
256 GoodGuide "GoodGuide Delivered to your Phone," http://www.goodguide.com/about/mobile#sms (accessed December 28, 2009).
257 Fairtrade Foundation, "Global Fairtrade Sales Increase by 22%," June 8, 2009, http://www.fairtrade.org.uk/press_office/press_releases_and_statements/jun_2009/global_fairtrade_sales_increase_by_22.aspx.
258 *Report on Trends in the North American Fair Trade Market* (Washington, DC: Fair Trade Federation, 2009), 4.
259 Carolyn Dallas (Executive Director, Time Dollar Youth Court), Personal Communication, January 18, 2005; For more information on time-dollar-type services, contact Time Dollar Youth Court, 409 East Street N.W., Building B, Washington, DC 20001, tel. (202) 508-1612, zfowlk@cs.com, http://www.timebanks.org.
260 "Facts on Folkbildning, A Brief Overview," Folkbildningsrådet, Stockholm, 2008, 2, http://

www.docstoc.com/docs/2319981/Facts-on-folkbildning-in-Sweden.

261 "Profiles of Successful Dialogue-to-Change Programs Strengthening Neighborhoods," Everyday Democracy, May 14, 2008, http://www.everyday-democracy.org/en/Article.295.aspx, (accessed August, 24, 2009); Nick Connell (Everyday Democracy), Personal Communication.

262 AmericaSpeaks, "Case Studies," http://americaspeaks.org/index.cfm?fuseaction=Page.viewPage&pageId=499&parentID=473.

263 Public Campaign, "Clean Elections Legislation Summary Summer 2007," http://library.publicampaign.org/sites/default/files/08-14-07_Clean_Elections_Summary.pdf.

264 You Street, "Success in the States," December 18, 2009, http://youstreet.org/states#arizona.

265 Small Planet Institute, "Getting a Grip on Money in Politics—Part I and II," http://www.smallplanet.org/Video/.

266 Public Campaign, "Clean Facts," http://www.publicampaign.org/clean-facts (accessed December 28, 2009).

267 Lake Research Partners, "Memorandum on Election Week Survey on Public Funding of Elections," November 12, 2008, http://otrans.3cdn.net/d2e5a66e63d9a5e39f_zqm6bhlaf.pdf.

268 FairVote, "Where Instant Run-Off Voting has Been Adopted," http://www.fairvote.org/where-instant-runoff-voting-has-been-adopted (accessed December 28, 2009).

269 FairVote, "How Instant Run-Off Voting Works," http://www.fairvote.org/how-instant-runoff-voting-works.

270 "Was the 2004 Election Stolen? Ohio's Missing Votes," *Rolling Stone Magazine*, http://www.rollingstone.com/photos/gallery/10467024/was_the_2004_election_stolen/photo/3.

271 Robert F. Kennedy, Jr., "Was the 2004 Election Stolen?," *Rolling Stone Magazine*, June 1, 2006, http://www.rollingstone.com/news/story/10432334/was_the_2004_election_stolen.

272 Paul Blumenthal, "How Congress Rushed a Bill that Helped Bring the Economy to its Knees," *Huffington Post*, May 11, 2009, http://www.huffingtonpost.com/paul-blumenthal/how-congress-rushed-a-bil_b_181926.html.

273 Barry Paris, "In 'Capitalism,' Michael Moore Proposes his Own New Deal," *Pittsburgh Post-Gazette*, October 2, 2009, http://www.post-gazette.com/pg/09275/1002407-120.stm; "Obama Blasts Wall Street; Is this Change?; Blagojevich Thrown out; Border Drug Violence," *Lou Dobbs Tonight*, January 29, 2009, http://edition.cnn.com/TRANSCRIPTS/0901/29/ldt.01.html.

274 M.J. Stephey, "Voices of the Iraq War: Senator Russ Feingold---Democrat," March 18, 2008, *Time Magazine*, http://www.time.com/time/world/article/0,8599,1723230-1,00.html; US Senator Russ Feingold "Listening Sessions," http://feingold.senate.gov/listening/index.html.

275 Nazila Fathi, "Iran Professors Ask for End of Violence, *New York Times*, January 4, 2010, http://www.nytimes.com/2010/01/05/world/middleeast/05iran.html.

# INDEX

## C

## G



## H

## N



## O



## P

## Q



## R



## S

## T

# OTHER SUGGESTED TITLES FROM FRANCES AND ANNA LAPPÉ

Bloomsbury (2009) ISBN 978-1-59691-659-3 / $24.00

## Diet for a Hot Planet

**The Climate Crisis at the End of Your Fork and What You Can Do About It**

by Anna Lappé

*"Anna Lappe's Diet for a Hot Planet does for the present generation what her mother's Diet for a Small Planet did for the last: empower us to think in a new way about how food affects our own health as well as that of the planet. Her inspiring book makes it clear that food choices matter to climate change and that each of us, voting with our forks, can make a real difference in ensuring a more sustainable food system. I want all my students to read this powerful book."*

—MARION NESTLE, Professor of Nutrition, Food Studies, and Public Health, New York University, and author of *What to Eat.*

Small Planet Media (2009) / ISBN: 978-0-9794142-1-3 $14.95
Visit **www.smallplanet.org** for details.

## Liberation Ecology (Fall 2010)

**Reframing Six Disempowering Ideas that Keep Us from Aligning with Nature- Even Our Own**

by Frances Moore Lappé

*"This book is brilliant...captivating, and powerful. It has already begun to change some of the ways I think about important issues."*

—ERIC ZAMOST, Business Consultant

*"...a real watershed. Not just in our thinking about certain things, like* Silent Spring *back in the '60s or* Diet for a Small Planet *in the '70s, but the beginning of a real paradigm shift in human civilization."*

—DAVE FORREST, Internet Entrepreneur

Ask your favorite bookseller or visit smallplanet.org

Tarcher (2003) / ISBN: 978-1585422371 / $14.95

## Hope's Edge

### The Next Diet for a Small Planet

**by Frances Moore Lappé, Anna Lappé**

*"Absolutely one of the most important books as we move further in the 21st century."*
—JANE GOODALL

*"Hope's Edge is not only a brilliant analysis of the global food and hunger challenge; it is also a philosophical work of the first order."*
—GEORGE MCGOVERN, UN Global Ambassador for Hunger

*"Passionate and wise ... Just the book we need now."* —ERIC SCHLOSSER, author of *Fast Food Nation*

Tarcher (2005) / ISBN: 978-1585424245 / $13.95

## You Have the Power

### Choosing Courage in a Culture of Fear

**by Frances Moore Lappé, Jeffrey Perkins**

*"Outwit the fearmongers. Read this gutsy gem!"*
—MICHAEL MOORE

*"... exhilarating jujitsu of a book ... liberating stuff."* —STUDS TERKEL

*"Challenging the 'official word' that has proclaimed fear an essential attribute of patriotism, Lappé... and Perkins share portraits of extraordinary, ordinary people who have overcome their personal fears."*
—*Library Journal*